QUALITY IMPLEMENTATION

QUALITY IMPLEMENTATION

LEVERAGING COLLECTIVE EFFICACY
TO MAKE "WHAT WORKS" ACTUALLY WORK

Jenni Donohoo and Steven Katz

FOR INFORMATION:

Corwin

A SAGE Company

2455 Teller Road

Thousand Oaks, California 91320

(800) 233-9936

www.corwin.com

SAGE Publications Ltd.

1 Oliver's Yard

55 City Road

London EC1Y 1SP

United Kingdom

SAGE Publications India Pvt. Ltd.

B 1/I 1 Mohan Cooperative Industrial Area

Mathura Road, New Delhi 110 044

India

SAGE Publications Asia-Pacific Pte. Ltd.

18 Cross Street #10-10/11/12

China Square Central

Singapore 048423

Program Director and Publisher: Dan Alpert

Content Development Editor: Lucas Schleicher

Senior Editorial Assistant: Mia Rodriguez

Production Editor: Tori Mirsadjadi

Copy Editor: Patrice Sutton

Typesetter: C&M Digitals (P) Ltd.

Proofreader: Liann Lech

Indexer: Nancy Fulton

Cover Designer: Anupama Krishnan

Marketing Manager: Sharon Pendergast

Printed in the United States of America

ISBN: 978-1-5443-5425-5

This book is printed on acid-free paper.

Certified Chain of Custody
Promoting Sustainable Forestry
www.sfiprogram.org
SFI-01268

SFI label applies to text stock

19 20 21 22 23 10 9 8 7 6 5 4 3 2 1

CONTENTS

PART II: FOSTERING BELIEFS TO REALIZE QUALITY IMPLEMENTATION

LIST OF FIGURES, TABLES, AND RESOURCES

PREFACE

Ray Navarro, a California fire chief, and his fellow firefighters always shared a strong conviction that they could succeed, despite all other circumstances. Navarro described how this worked to their advantage during a particular rescue that he and his team will never forget. It was a nearly impossible situation they encountered on January 12, 2012, when they were called to the scene of an accident on Highway 101 in Buellton, California. Kelli Groves, a second-grade teacher, and her two daughters were in a horrific automobile crash. The BMW that Kelli was driving was so badly crushed, it was barely recognizable.

> *"People who have high collective efficacy will mobilize their efforts and resources to surmount the obstacles to the changes they seek"* (Bandura, 1998, p. 69).

Kelli was traveling to San Francisco with her ten-week-old daughter in a rear car seat and her ten-year-old daughter in the backseat next to her infant sister when a semitruck ran over the car, damaging it so badly, it seemed impossible that anyone could have survived. In our interview with Ray Navarro, he described how the firefighting team put their training and practice to use as the team got into "operational mode." Below, Ray described how the team stayed focused, relied on their training, and worked interdependently during the two-hour rescue operation.

"I recall when arriving on the incident and scene, we had three different things that were going on at the time. We had a semitruck that had demolished Kelli's BMW. The semitruck went over the highway where there was a gap between two bridges, fell one hundred feet, and exploded into flames. Unfortunately, the driver had perished. Hazardous materials had spilled from the truck, and we have this car dangling off a bridge by a tire with people inside. Kelli could feel the heat from the flames coming up the cavern between the two bridges and informed us her daughters were in the backseat. We were also dealing with a traffic jam and a road closure on a major freeway.

"With that," Ray continued, "arriving on the scene, the acting captain made a call for more help. He asked for more resources because originally the call had been sent out as a single engine call. We knew we had to access additional resources and then use them to the best advantage. In other words, we placed people in positions where they needed to be.

"It was my responsibility to develop teams: a cutting team, a stabilizing team, a paramedic team, and another team to stand by because we still had a fire underneath us and the BMW had gasoline in it, so we also needed a rescue team with extinguishment. From the team aspect, we looked at this and said we have to divide ourselves up to get the job done. Our emphasis to Kelli was 'We're going to get all of you out. It's going to take a while but we're going to do this.' As a team, we didn't have to say what our job was, we just did it, and that came as the result of practice and training" (R. Navarro, interview, October 18, 2017).

Ray noted that as the firefighters were reassuring Kelli, they were getting no response from her children. He continued to describe what they did next. "We needed to steady the vehicle, so we got a rope and used a tow truck as an anchor in an attempt to stabilize Kelli's car. I remember looking at one of our firefighters whose only job was to watch the rope. I saw him kneeling with a constant eye on the rope. If we lost any tension, he would call out to us. It might have seemed like an unimportant job, just kneeling there, but it was one of the most integral parts of teamwork. We had men on top of that BMW and if the rope slackened, their safety was in jeopardy" (R. Navarro, interview, 2017).

Kelli's oldest daughter was enveloped in the car with metal all around her. Ray and his team had to peel the pieces of metal off of her in order to get to her; they could hear her moaning from her injuries. Ray noted that "we just went to work. Kelli and her children became part of our team, and we reassured her of that telling her 'we're not going to let anyone go!' When you make it personal to yourself, you leave no one behind" (R. Navarro, interview, 2017). Ray noted that Kelli and her daughters were what made their rescue team relevant and that they weren't going to fail because if they failed Kelli and her girls, they failed themselves.

In what Ray described as a "divine moment," the team was approached by drivers of a military truck with an arm-like crane. The truck had broken down only moments before the accident happened. The crane was able to provide the stability needed to free Kelli and her daughters from the wreck. Ray reflected on the significance of this. He noted, "Others, who belonged to a different discipline—these were naval guys—had the tool we needed, and their instinct was to help" (R. Navarro, interview, 2017). With the help of the extended team, Kelli and her daughters were freed from the wreck and airlifted to a hospital in Santa Barbara. They all fully recovered from their injuries.

Ray shared with us a final thought from his team's successful experience in what he referred to as "The Bridge Incident." He said that there was an urgency to reopen the highway but that in the midst of everything, the team needed to pause. Ray asked for ten minutes, gathered the team in a circle, and acknowledged the incredible job that everyone did in saving three lives. He said that after the wave of emotion that was going to take over, he knew the team would need to debrief so that they would have a better understanding of what took place.

The Bridge Incident is an example of how confidence in the power of the collective helps teams overcome extraordinary obstacles. When recounting the events, Ray noted, "It was never our focus that we couldn't do this. It was our watch, as a team, we knew we could do what it would take to keep Kelli and her daughters safe" (R. Navarro, interview, 2017). Key elements of the teams' success included that they were well trained in the best practices required to get the job done, they were able to execute these practices in response to the task they faced, and they adjusted their strategies accordingly. The team was coordinated and relied on each other in jointly interdependent ways. Most importantly, they shared the belief that *they could succeed*. This example shows the power of collective efficacy—the belief that a team can accomplish its goals despite difficult circumstances.

This book is about the power of collective efficacy in schools. Collective efficacy refers to educators' shared beliefs that through their combined efforts they can positively influence student outcomes, including outcomes for those who are disengaged, unmotivated, and/or disadvantaged. Collective efficacy is a significant belief system for improving student outcomes. When educators share the belief that they can influence student achievement, regardless of some of the difficult circumstances faced in schools today, the results can be very powerful. In fact, research shows that collective efficacy matters more in relation to increasing student achievement than the neighborhoods where students come from and their level of household income (Donohoo, Hattie, & Eells, 2018). That is not to say that demographic characteristics are irrelevant—they are relevant! These things matter; however, what educator teams do to create a better environment for student learning has a clear, measurable, and greater impact on student achievement than do demographic variables. This book is about the power of educator teams in overcoming challenges and obstacles. It is about the important contributions that educators make to students' lives over and above the impact of students' homes and communities.

Collective efficacy influences student achievement because greater efficacy drives behaviors that are instrumental to quality implementation. Quality implementation is a process through which evidence-based promises of improvement-oriented interventions get realized in practice. In the first half of this book, readers will find examples of how educators' beliefs affect thought patterns in ways that either support or hinder quality implementation. Using examples from both inside and outside of education, readers will learn how an established sense of collective efficacy helps teams figure out ways to make *what's supposed to work* actually work given their unique environments. Efficacious teams find ways to exercise control over the challenges that surround them. They also exert greater effort and muster up the strength, motivation, and resolve needed in order to meet challenging goals (as evidenced in The Bridge Incident). Conversely, teams who lack collective efficacy become preoccupied by constraints, show significant reduction in the goals they set, and lower their efforts. Readers will find examples of how the consequences of a reduced sense of collective efficacy impede quality implementation in schools.

In the second half of this book, we identify factors that influence a team's interpretation of their effectiveness and outline what educator teams can do to strengthen efficacy-shaping sources. Since successful performance accomplishments are the most significant source of collective efficacy, we share key features of mastery experiences and discuss what teams can focus on in order to create mastery environments. We also examine ways to strengthen vicarious experiences through observational learning. In the final chapter, we discuss two additional sources of collective efficacy, social persuasion and affective states, and consider how teams could use theories of persuasion in order to capitalize on persuasion as an efficacy-enhancing source. Each chapter finishes with a section headed "Time for Reflection," which presents a number of questions relating to the main ideas in the chapter. These questions are designed to help readers reflect on and mobilize the content in each chapter in a personal way.

We conclude by encouraging readers to examine the conceptual framework (see Figure 1) we developed. This conceptual framework maps the ideas and relationships among the concepts contained in this book. A key finding from cognitive science is that in order to develop competence in an area of inquiry, learners must understand facts and ideas in the context of a conceptual framework (Bransford, Brown, & Cocking, 2000). Our aim is to help educators realize quality implementation by directly utilizing the knowledge gained from reading this book. Therefore, the conceptual framework is offered as a strategy to encourage transfer.

School improvement depends upon the collective belief that the teaching faculty has what it takes to improve student achievement. If we want to realize the promise of improvement-oriented interventions, one of the most important things we can do is equip teacher teams with the confidence that they have what it takes to improve outcomes for students. The purpose of this book is to help teams achieve quality implementation of evidence-based practices by fostering a sense of collective efficacy. When efficacy is firmly established, educators go outside their comfort zones; use focused, goal-driven activity to improve an area of weakness; and make changes based on feedback received. Theory and practice are brought together in a way that is mediated by context. The result of quality implementation is innovative and lasting change that becomes accepted practice and produces positive outcomes.

ABOUT THE AUTHORS

Jenni Donohoo is the director of Praxis-Engaging Ideas, Inc. and a project manager for the Council of Ontario Directors of Education (CODE). Jenni has a PhD in educational studies and supervisory officer qualifications. Jenni is a former classroom teacher and currently works with systems, school leaders, and teachers around the world to support high-quality professional learning. She has authored many peer-reviewed publications and three best-selling books: *Collaborative Inquiry for Educators, The Transformative Power of Collaborative Inquiry* (with Moses Velasco), and *Collective Efficacy: How Educators' Beliefs Impact Student Learning.* Jenni's areas of expertise include collective efficacy, metacognition, adolescent literacy, and facilitating collaborative learning structures.

Steven Katz is the director of Aporia Consulting Ltd. and a faculty member in Applied Psychology and Human Development at the Ontario Institute for Studies in Education of the University of Toronto (OISE, UT), where he teaches in the Child Study and Education graduate program. He is the recipient of the OISE, UT-wide award for teaching excellence. Steven has a PhD in human development and applied psychology, with specialization in applied cognitive science. His areas of expertise include cognition and learning, teacher education, networked learning communities, leading professional learning, and evidence-informed decision making for school improvement. He has received the Governor General's Medal for excellence in his field and has been involved in research and evaluation, professional development, and consulting with a host of educational organizations around the world. He is the author of several best-selling books, including *Leading Schools in a Data-Rich World; Building and Connecting Learning Communities; Intentional Interruption;* and *The Intelligent, Responsive Leader.*

Figure 1 Conceptual Framework—Quality Implementation: Leveraging Collective Efficacy to Make "What Works" Actually Work

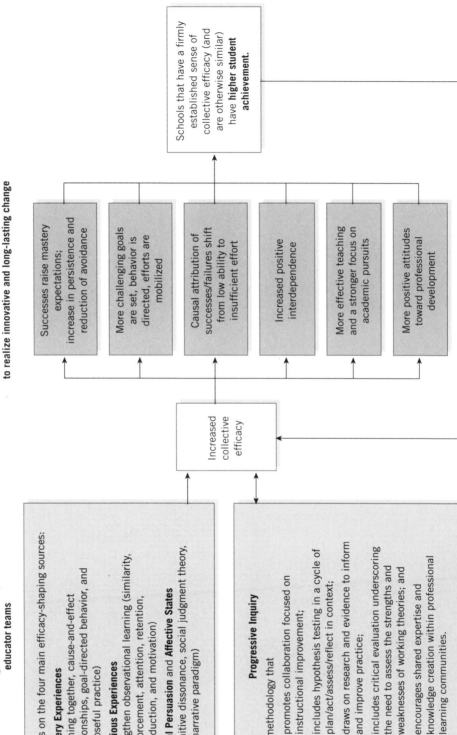

Fostering collective efficacy with educator teams

Consequences: achieve quality implementation to realize innovative and long-lasting change

Focus on the four main efficacy-shaping sources:

Mastery Experiences
(learning together, cause-and-effect relationships, goal-directed behavior, and purposeful practice)

Vicarious Experiences
strengthen observational learning (similarity, reinforcement, attention, retention, reproduction, and motivation)

Social Persuasion and **Affective States**
(cognitive dissonance, social judgment theory, and narrative paradigm)

Progressive Inquiry

A methodology that

- promotes collaboration focused on instructional improvement;
- includes hypothesis testing in a cycle of plan/act/assess/reflect in context;
- draws on research and evidence to inform and improve practice;
- includes critical evaluation underscoring the need to assess the strengths and weaknesses of working theories; and
- encourages shared expertise and knowledge creation within professional learning communities.

Increased collective efficacy

Successes raise mastery expectations; increase in persistence and reduction of avoidance

More challenging goals are set, behavior is directed, efforts are mobilized

Causal attribution of successes/failures shift from low ability to insufficient effort

Increased positive interdependence

More effective teaching and a stronger focus on academic pursuits

More positive attitudes toward professional development

Schools that have a firmly established sense of collective efficacy (and are otherwise similar) have **higher student achievement.**

BELIEFS AS THE FOUNDATION TO QUALITY IMPLEMENTATION

THE ELUSIVE QUEST FOR QUALITY IMPLEMENTATION

A Failed Attempt at Spreading Evidence-Based Practices

A few years ago, Natalie, a director of professional learning in a small school district, attended a conference. In one of the breakout sessions, she learned about the concept of restorative practice. Educators from a neighboring district were sharing how they had put restorative practices into place in their schools to address bullying behavior. They had documented evidence of how restorative practices were resulting in more supportive learning environments and shared videos and research that demonstrated its effectiveness as an approach to conflict resolution. Natalie found this concept intriguing because she knew that reducing bullying and promoting responsible behavior remained a focus in many of the high schools in her district.

She immediately arranged for experienced trainers from a national restorative practices organization to share information at an upcoming principals' meeting. In the next phase of training, Natalie asked school administrators to identify teacher leaders and invite them to a series of full-day sessions to learn about restorative circles and other restorative approaches that could be used to resolve relationship-damaging incidents in schools.

It was an expensive endeavor. The costs for the travel and presentation fees for experienced trainers consumed a large portion of Natalie's professional learning budget. Additional monies covered the cost of occasional teachers, rental fees for the hall where the training took place, and the cost of breakfast and lunch for the attendees. In four of the six high schools, some follow-through occurred immediately after each professional learning session. In three of the four schools where initial uptake seemed promising, some of the practices continued into the next school year. Within a few months, however, restorative justice was not practiced to a large extent in any of the high schools. In fact, it was not carried out at all.

Many well-intentioned educators have probably had similar experiences and can relate to the above example. An approach to school improvement (in this case restorative practices)—supported by research and achieving results in other locations—is introduced into schools but fails to live up to its potential. The practice of restorative justice could be substituted for any number of promising interventions with the same outcome. Simply introducing evidence-based approaches into schools does not guarantee they will be implemented meaningfully over time.

> *Simply introducing evidence-based approaches into schools does not guarantee they will be implemented meaningfully over time.*

School improvement initiatives often miss the mark in achieving the innovative and long-lasting changes needed to positively impact success for all students. It would not be difficult for most educators to name *several change initiatives* that were introduced but never came to fruition in the duration of their careers. Identifying ones that actually took hold would be a more challenging task. Even mandated change, in the form of policy, does not guarantee uptake in schools and classrooms.

We Already Know What's "Supposed" to Work in Schools

We are on fairly solid ground when it comes to the *what* of school improvement. A plethora of research about what works in schools dates back many decades. There are also many books and resources designed to assist busy educators in sifting through the research in an effort to make it more accessible and applicable to their practice. Over fifteen years have passed since Robert Marzano's (2003) *What Works in Schools: Translating Research into Action* was published. Marzano synthesized thirty-five years of research in order to identify what was known about the factors that affect student achievement and noted that schools could have a "tremendous impact on student achievement if they follow the direction provided by research" (p. 4). He also suggested that educators were up to the challenge of *implementing* what we know about effective schooling.

More recently, John Hattie has gained worldwide recognition based on his life's hobby in which he synthesized major findings from over 1500 meta-analyses that investigated factors that influence student achievement. Hattie (2009) demonstrated the magnitude and overall distribution of more than 150,000 effect sizes so that practitioners could compare influences in a meaningful way and use evidence to build and defend a model for teaching and learning. Hattie's (2009) major purpose was to "generate a model of successful teaching and learning based on the many thousands of studies" (p. 237). He noted, however, that "the practice of teaching has changed little over the past century" (p. 5).

Even though the available research points educators in the right direction, quality implementation of evidence-based strategies remains a consistent and widespread challenge when it comes to school improvement efforts.

"While we collect evidence, teachers go on teaching" (Hattie, 2009, p. 5).

Quality Implementation Defined

We define quality implementation as a process through which the evidence-based promises of improvement-oriented interventions get realized in practice. The process involves a critical mass of people in any given organization doing their best to apply and experiment with *what's supposed to work*, assessing impact relative to the intended outcomes, learning about what worked and what did not work and why within respective contexts, and then making the necessary modifications accordingly. In short, quality implementation is the epitome of a progressive inquiry methodology. We will provide specific details about structures that complement a progressive inquiry methodology later in this book. For now, note that when engaging in progressive inquiry, educators "go outside their comfort zones, use focused, goal-driven activity to improve an area of weakness, and make changes based on feedback received" (Katz, Dack, & Malloy, 2018, p. 66). Theory and practice are brought together in a way that is mediated by context. Quality implementation results in innovative and lasting change that becomes accepted practice and produces positive outcomes.

Essential Aspects of a Progressive Inquiry Methodology

- Inquiry is driven by the team's authentic desire to gain a better understanding of how to address student learning needs within their particular school and classrooms.

- Working theories are constructed and made public so that assumptions can be surfaced and theories can be evaluated in light of evidence.

- Searching for and working with evidence-based strategies is necessary for deepening collective understandings.

- A critical condition for progress is that inquirers focus on improving their practice by generating more specific questions and searching for new information.

- Knowledge is created not by individuals but by individuals embedded in a community, or even the community itself.

The Problem of Getting
to Quality Implementation

As mentioned earlier, the problem with school improvement is less in the *what* than in the *how*—in *doing* what needs to be done—and *sticking with it* long enough to figure out how it can work for a critical mass of practitioners within specific contexts. Quality implementation has always been a major barrier to successful educational reform. Unfortunately, the changes needed to positively impact success for all students cannot be realized without it. Such attainment requires implementation.

The problem of achieving quality implementation is not unique to the field of education. In the health care system, a wealth of empirical evidence exists, gleaned from randomized controlled experiments and reports, about what works best based on evidence. Even though there is high-quality evidence regarding the value of new clinical interventions, the transfer-to-practice rate is very slow. Reports demonstrate that evidence-based practices can take an average of seventeen years to be incorporated into routine general practice in health care, and less than 50 percent gets incorporated at all (Balas & Boren, 2000).

In a review that examined the rate of transfer of evidence-based practices into routine use in health care, Balas and Boren (2000) argued that more needed to be done to put well-substantiated recommendations into clinical practice. The authors cite evidence showing that it took thirteen years—after publications indicating that clot-busting drugs (known as thrombolytic drugs) could be used to effectively treat dangerous clots in blood vessels, improve blood flow, and prevent damage to tissues and organs—for experts to recommend them in the treatment of heart attacks.

> Balas and Boren (2000) noted that back in 1843, Oliver Wendell Holmes read the first of his famous papers on the "contagiousness of puerperal fever" (a fever caused by uterine infection following childbirth). He advised that physicians wash their hands before examining pregnant women as a means of preventing the infection from spreading. This radical change in practice at that time met with resistance. Balas and Boren pointed out that it took *decades* for Holmes's suggestion to become universally accepted and applied in health care practice.

Barriers occur at the various stages whereby an intervention moves from clinical research to sustained application in general health care practice. The main issue in health care is in applying evidence-based practices in less controlled settings than the laboratories in which the practices were initially tested. Attempting to apply procedures in different environments can lead to quality gaps that impede the uptake (Bauer, Damschroder, Hagedorn, Smith, & Kilbourne, 2015). Explicit contrasts remain between implementing programs in the "real world" and "controlled research environments" where factors can be controlled in health care (Lindland, Fond, Haydon, Volmert, & Kendall-Taylor, 2015). In other words, context matters!

Attempting to apply procedures in different environments can lead to quality gaps that impede the uptake.

Even though most educational research does not take place in controlled laboratory settings, the same issues arise when educators attempt to apply what is known from research in different school environments. Complex contextual factors impede uptake. Applying strategies in different contexts can create quality gaps. Even though an intervention worked somewhere for somebody, what we do not know is what it will take to make it work for different subgroups of students and teachers across a variety of contexts (Katz, Dack, & Malloy, 2018). Unfortunately, not all change efforts are designed in ways that lead to quality implementation because they fail to account for the complex contextual factors that are unique in each school environment.

Implications or consequences result from the lag between applying what is known from research findings and putting it into everyday practice in meaningful ways. For example, the implications of evidence-based practices taking up to seventeen years before becoming routine use in health care systems remain enormous; and in schools, the slow rate of transfer has high-stakes implications as well. It is not just an interesting observation, for the consequences are best understood in terms of a moral imperative. The longer educators wait, the more difficult it is to close achievement gaps. In order to ensure success for all students, it is incumbent upon educators to take what is known from educational research and find ways to apply it meaningfully in the context of their school environments. Through the process of progressive inquiry, theory and practice are brought together in a way that is mediated by context enabling better quality implementation.

Implementing change in schools is as complex an undertaking as implementing evidence-based practices in health care. One might expect that student achievement would incrementally increase in relation to the number of educators who adopt each new initiative; but that is not the case. Reeves (2008) demonstrated that the relationship between implementation and school improvement is not a linear one. In other words, schools cannot expect a change in outcomes until the *majority* of teachers put new strategies into practice.

Schools cannot expect a change in outcomes until initiatives are implemented by the majority of teachers.

An All Too Familiar Case of Failed Implementation

Andrew's experience, shared below, might be all too familiar to readers. Andrew, an administrator of an elementary school, oversees a faculty of twenty-five teachers. A few years ago, program coordinators from the district office introduced a writing program that focused on six traits of writing: ideas, organization, fluency, voice, conventions, and word choice. There were opportunities for teachers to attend learning sessions where this new approach to teaching writing was introduced. Resources including kits and blackline masters were provided for every teacher in Andrew's school. Andrew attended the professional development, along with his teachers, and felt that by focusing on the traits of writing, as suggested by the district literacy consultants, the school's writing results would improve over time.

That was not the case, however. Writing scores remained stagnant at Andrew's school for the first year following the introduction of the writing program. As a result, Andrew requested further learning opportunities for his teachers and purchased additional resources, including student writing notebooks. A few keen teachers, upon receiving the initial training and materials, immediately began to use them in their classrooms. A few more were on board after attending the additional learning sessions. However, at the end of the second year, writing scores still showed no improvement. Even though there was now very little support being provided from the district in relation to the writing program, Andrew allocated funds for the purchase of additional resources including posters, anchor charts, and online tutorials in an effort to ensure teachers had the materials they needed. After the third year, there were still no measurable gains. With only a moderate degree of implementation, the evidence-based writing program had no impact on student results. Less than half of Andrew's faculty actually implemented the writing program with fidelity in their classrooms.

Doug Reeves's (2008) research confirms the lesson that we can take away from Andrew's experience. Measurable gains in student learning cannot be realized until deep levels of implementation are reached. In examining the degree of teacher implementation of *Five Easy Steps to a Balanced Math Program* and math scores in fifteen schools in the state of Indiana, Reeves concluded that significant increases in student results did not occur *until* the majority of the faculty implemented the program. The percentage of students scoring proficient or higher on statewide tests did not change when teachers reported "seldom" or "moderate" use of the new strategies for teaching mathematics. Reeves (2008) reached the same conclusions when examining math and language arts scores and the implementation of *assessment for learning*. He suggested that the adoption of initiatives among 90 percent or more of the faculty is the threshold if we want to see changes resulting in measurable outcomes for students.

> *Measurable gains in student learning cannot be realized until deep levels of implementation are reached.*

In the preceding examples, the evidence-based programs or the teaching approaches themselves, such as *assessment for learning*, should not be criticized. The problem lies in the lack of quality implementation. As we have seen, schools cannot expect to realize gains in student outcomes until the *majority* of teachers put new strategies into practice. However, it is an oversimplification to assume that the key to quality implementation rests solely on gaining critical mass. As we noted, quality implementation is the process through which evidence-based promises of improvement-oriented interventions get realized in practice—that is, getting a critical mass of people to step outside of their comfort zone by applying, experimenting, and using feedback in order to make improvements in an area of need. Therefore, quality implementation involves a multidimensional conception of scale. When thinking about how to achieve innovative and lasting change, we need to look beyond the number of educators involved and consider other dimensions of scale as well.

> *It is an oversimplification to assume that the key to quality implementation rests solely on gaining critical mass.*

Beliefs Matter

Cynthia Coburn (2003) challenged traditional notions of what it means to "scale up" educational change efforts and suggested that scale has four inter-related dimensions: depth, sustainability, spread, and shift in reform ownership. In addition to considering the number of people or schools involved (spread), Coburn encouraged educators and researchers to also think about the nature of the change (depth), the degree to which it is sustained (sustainability), and the degree to which educators have the knowledge and authority to grow the reform over time (ownership) when defining scale.

Coburn (2003) referred to sustainability as the degree to which changes become ongoing habits of teachers and school practices. She also noted that the change must be owned, understood, and put into action internally, rather than externally. When considering depth, Coburn (2003) noted that change requires deep and lasting learning for both educators and students, and change and deep learning occur with *transformational shifts in educators' beliefs.*

These dimensions of scale provide us a way to think about quality implementation. As noted earlier, the result of quality implementation is innovative and lasting change that becomes accepted practice. Realizing there are better ways to do things, accepting new practices and making them permanent, is really about changing one's fundamental beliefs. This comes as a result of engaging in progressive inquiry. Deep learning that leads to *transformational shifts in beliefs* occurs as educators come to better understand the nature of the change, persist in sustaining the change, and develop confidence in regard to their ability to grow it in their own school environments. In this sense, depth, sustainability, spread, and ownership are characteristics of quality implementation achieved through cycles of progressive inquiry.

Unfortunately, not all change efforts are designed in ways that lead to a realization of these characteristics of quality implementation because in addition to failing to account for complex contextual factors, they fail to account for misguided beliefs as well. Whether beliefs are about low expectations, faulty attributions for students' successes and failures, or a diminished sense of what the team is able to collectively accomplish, when beliefs remain unexamined or unchallenged, it can lead to behaviors that are counterproductive to students' success, as demonstrated in the following example.

An Attempt at Integrating Literacy Instruction in High School Content-Area Classrooms

Years ago, one of us conducted research in two high schools, examining the impact of content-area literacy instruction on student learning. Many adolescents struggle with reading and writing in subject-specific disciplines and present different challenges from those of younger students. Proficiency in these areas is a critical determinant of students' overall success in school. Students who have not acquired sufficient skills in reading and writing by the end of elementary school will be limited in their ability to comprehend high school content-area texts. Unfortunately, as the content and texts become more challenging, literacy instruction is often limited or nonexistent in many science, history, geography, and other content-area classes.

High school teachers experience difficulty integrating reading and writing strategies into their daily instruction for a variety of reasons. They feel they do not have the time to teach both the content of their subject and literacy strategies. They see it as an added task, one relatively low on their list of priorities. Many content-area teachers are reluctant to think of themselves as teachers of reading and writing and believe that literacy instruction remains the responsibility of the English department. In reality, content-area teachers have not been properly trained to address students' literacy needs, and they collectively lack the confidence that they are able to do so.

An intervention program titled Think Literacy aimed to enhance the implementation of reading and writing strategies in ninth-grade science, mathematics, and geography classes in two high schools. In addition to numerous professional development sessions provided by program coordinators at the school district, teachers were provided with common preparation time, instructional coaches, and additional resources. Teachers attended full-day professional learning sessions with internationally recognized experts in adolescent literacy, and the instructional coaches provided follow-up support. Administrators were present at most of the learning sessions and supported teachers as well. Instructional coaches had an abundance of professional learning opportunities in order to ensure they were equipped to provide effective coaching and on-site support. Even though some of the teachers were initially a bit reluctant, it *seemed* like all the requirements necessary for successful implementation were in place.

However, results from the research revealed that even after three years of intense support, the intervention was not implemented to the degree needed to impact student results. Teachers failed to embed critical components of effective strategy instruction into their practice. The majority of teachers continued to teach the same way they had prior to being introduced to evidence-based strategies that yielded high potential to impact student learning. With the introduction of each new strategy, teachers initially tried it in their classrooms but abandoned each almost immediately.

It helps to understand the failure of this project through the lens of quality implementation. The majority of teachers were not involved (the project targeted only ninth-grade teachers). Also, teachers who were involved implemented only some of the strategies, some of the time. They did not reach a level where the strategies were sustained over time, and a shift in reform ownership did not take place. This is because the change strategy failed to account for the power of teachers' beliefs in influencing their practice.

The change strategy failed to account for the power of teachers' beliefs in influencing their practice.

The program specifically targeted teachers responsible for applied classes because results from standardized tests indicated this group of students was most at-risk. Students enrolled in applied courses are usually headed on a pathway toward the workplace. They are typically not university bound. What makes addressing the literacy needs of students who are enrolled in applied classes particularly challenging is that students often hold low expectations of themselves. Unfortunately, some teachers hold low expectations of students in applied courses as well.

An instructional coach at one of the schools recounted a conversation she had with one of the teachers while he calculated his average class marks on his midterm report cards. He taught both an academic (university-bound) and an applied (workplace-bound) geography class and realized that the midterm average for the students in the applied class was higher than the average for students in the academic class. Even though the class size was smaller in the applied course and the applied curriculum was designed to focus more on application and hands-on activities, the higher average obtained by students in the applied class left him with an uneasy feeling. He expressed his concerns to the instructional coach, indicating that students in applied classes *should not* be doing better than the university-bound students. He made adjustments to the grades in order to resolve this perceived discrepancy. He lowered the grades for each student in his applied class until the average for the class was less than the average obtained by students in his academic class.

In addition to low expectations held by teachers and students, teachers involved in this project often attributed students' failures to factors that were outside of their control. Many complained that students were not engaged and that parents were unsupportive. One of the schools was located in an area with low socioeconomic status and a high percentage of single-parent households. Teachers were quick to deflect blame to external sources, indicating that there was very little they could do to impact student achievement if students were not motivated to do their schoolwork and if parents did not show concern over their sons' and daughters' late or missing assignments. These entrenched beliefs were the biggest barrier to implementation.

> *Often, entrenched beliefs are a large barrier to implementation efforts in schools and school districts.*

Educators' Beliefs

One misguided belief, commonly held among educators, is that they lack the collective capability to impact the lives of their students over and above the influence of students' homes and communities. Collective efficacy refers to "the judgments of teachers in a school that the faculty as a whole can organize and execute the courses of action required to have a positive effect on students" (Goddard, Hoy, & Woolfolk Hoy, 2004, p. 4). As seen in the above example, when lacking collective efficacy, educators attribute failure to factors that are outside of their influence.

A lack of collective efficacy stifles quality implementation because it affects behavior in negative ways. School improvement initiatives are unlikely to be adopted unless administrators believe they have the knowledge and skills to execute them well and support teachers where needed. Likewise, new strategies and approaches are unlikely to be implemented in classrooms unless teams of teachers believe they have the skills and capabilities to put them into practice and the ability to provide support to students where needed (T. Guskey, personal communication, 2018).

> *When educators lack collective efficacy, the barriers to quality implementation are enormous.*

When collective efficacy is lacking, innovative and lasting change is unlikely. This is because limiting beliefs that remain unexamined or unchallenged result in behaviors that are counterproductive to students' success (as demonstrated in the example above). Beliefs are foundational to quality implementation. Quality implementation is defined by recursive cycles of progressive inquiry in which educators try something, use feedback to revise their approaches, try again, and so on, in order to realize the promise of evidence-based practices in specific contexts. It involves discomfort, effort, and perseverance. Without the beliefs, the "work" of quality implementation will not unfold. However, as the gap between theory and practice is being resolved through progressive inquiry, changes in beliefs and values evolve over time. We will explore this relationship and the essential elements of progressive inquiry in greater detail later in this book. We will also highlight professional learning structures that live within a progressive inquiry methodology.

In Conclusion

Successful educational reforms are defined by quality implementation of what is known to work best in systems, schools, and classrooms. You know you have quality implementation when you see depth, sustainability, spread, and shift in reform ownership. In education, this is rarely achieved. Even though a plethora of research exists that can point educators in promising directions, evidence-based strategies rarely get put into practice in ways that effect meaningful change. A number of contextual factors impact the uptake of research into practice. Most importantly, entrenched beliefs are a barrier to quality implementation efforts in schools and school districts. As we saw in the example of failed implementation of literacy instruction in content-area classrooms, certain situations cannot be adequately addressed within the context of the faculty's current beliefs and values. In our work in districts and schools, we know that shifting beliefs is contextual, difficult work and does not happen overnight. It is an adaptive challenge for which there is no algorithm, and it is core to the work of quality implementation.

When collective efficacy is present, educators are more likely to persist regardless of the tensions associated with balancing individual and collective autonomy. They are more likely to scale educational change efforts because they have the confidence in their combined ability to successfully execute the change. Collective efficacy drives the right kinds of behaviors that are instrumental to quality implementation. A lack of efficacy hinders progress. The relationship between collective efficacy and quality implementation, specifically how educators' beliefs affect thought patterns and behaviors in ways that either support or obstruct quality implementation, is explored in the following two chapters.

TIME FOR REFLECTION

1. What are you and your team currently working on in your practice as educators? How is your team trying to improve?

2. Select one or two evidence-based practices that are part of your team's improvement strategy. When considering the four interrelated dimensions of scale (depth, sustainability, spread, and shift in reform ownership), what are some strengths and what are areas for improvement?

3. What concepts in this chapter does your team want to know more about? What questions does your team have related to these concepts?

CHAPTER 2

WHY IMPLEMENTATION FREQUENTLY FAILS

As we saw in Chapter 1, school improvement initiatives often miss the mark in achieving long-lasting changes needed to positively impact student success. Implementing evidence-based approaches into everyday practice has been problematic partially because efforts to apply strategies in different contexts hinder quality implementation; entrenched beliefs often pose a large barrier to implementation efforts. Beliefs are contextual and based on assumptions teams of educators hold true in particular situations and environments. When it comes to successful school improvement, a faculty's belief that its members cannot foster the conditions necessary to impact student learning poses the most dangerous of these entrenched beliefs.

> When it comes to successful school improvement, a faculty's belief that its members cannot foster the conditions necessary to impact student learning poses the most dangerous of these entrenched beliefs.

Collective Efficacy

We introduced the concept of collective efficacy in the previous chapter. The term was coined by Albert Bandura, a psychologist at Stanford University, who studied the relationship between confidence levels and success. Bandura found that the more confident teams felt about their combined abilities, the more successful their performance. Bandura defined collective efficacy as "a group's shared belief in its conjoint capability to organize and execute the courses of action required to produce given levels of attainment" (Bandura, 1997, p. 476). The relationship between collective efficacy and results has been established in research in multiple domains as diverse as sports, business, and neighborhood crime.

The relationship between collective efficacy and better results also exists in schools. Collective *teacher* efficacy refers to educators' shared beliefs that through their combined efforts they can positively influence student outcomes, including those of students who are disengaged, unmotivated, and/or disadvantaged (Donohoo, 2017). It is the "collective self-perception

> "Collective efficacy perceptions are future-oriented beliefs about the functioning of a collective in a specific situation or context" (Moolenaar, Sleegers, & Daly, 2012, p. 253).

that teachers in a given school make an educational difference to their students over and above the educational impact of their homes and communities" (Tschannen-Moran & Barr, 2004, p. 190). When educators share a sense of efficacy, it results in greater effort, optimism and hope, commitment to challenging goals, and increased motivation.

We will see throughout this book that collective efficacy is a significant belief system for improving student outcomes. In fact, collective teacher efficacy is what matters *most* in raising student achievement. Research shows that collective efficacy matters more in relation to increasing student achievement than the neighborhoods where students come from and their level of household income. Bandura (1993) was the first to generate interest in this area by demonstrating that the effect of collective teacher efficacy on student achievement was stronger than the link between socioeconomic status and student achievement. Consistent findings have been reported in a number of other studies since (Donohoo, 2018). For example, Roger Goddard and colleagues (Goddard, Goddard, Kim, & Miller, 2015) examined the relationship between collective efficacy and student achievement and found that the more robust the sense of collective teacher efficacy, "the greater their levels of student achievement, even after controlling for school and student background characteristics and prior levels of student achievement" (p. 525).

> Collective efficacy is a significant belief system for improving student outcomes.

Rachel Eells (2011) conducted the first meta-analysis, synthesizing all available and relevant studies, to quantify the correlation between collective teacher efficacy and student achievement. Eells concluded that "the beliefs that teachers hold about the ability of the school as a whole to promote positive outcomes were predictive of positive learning outcomes for their students" (p. 115). As a result of Eells's research, collective teacher efficacy was positioned at the top of John Hattie's list of factors that influence student achievement, based on his synthesis of over 1500 meta-analyses (Donohoo, Hattie, & Eells, 2018). According to Hattie's Visible Learning[plus] research, collective teacher efficacy proved greater than three times more predictive of student achievement than socioeconomic status (2017, pp. 1–2). It is more than double the effect of prior achievement and more than triple the effect of home environment and parental involvement.

Conversely, negative consequences occur when collective efficacy is lacking. Less efficacious teams produce poorer results. Teams do not pursue courses of action because they doubt they can do what it takes to succeed. Whatever benefits options may hold, when collective efficacy diminishes, teams do not regard possibilities worthy of consideration. Decisions are largely based on efficacy judgments without weighing costs and benefits of available options (Bandura, 1998).

In schools, a lack of collective teacher efficacy results in unproductive thoughts and inactivity that, in turn, translate into underperformance. Underperformance leads to poor results that further diminish collective efficacy, creating a downward spiral in which collective efficacy continues to decrease as implementation and results decline.

> *"Unless people believe they can produce desired effects by their actions they have little incentive to act" (Bandura, 1998, p. 52).*

A team's belief in their efficacy influences the anticipatory scenarios and futures they visualize (Bandura, 1998). Those who doubt their combined ability visualize failure scenarios that undermine implementation. When a faculty lacks a sense of efficacy they are less resourceful, and when faced with difficult challenges, teams slacken their efforts and settle for mediocre solutions.

Diminished Efficacy Is a Barrier to Quality Implementation

When collective efficacy is diminished, it can be a major barrier to quality implementation. In the previous chapter, we noted that quality implementation is characterized by a critical mass of educators, understanding, owning, and putting changes into place to the degree in which they become ongoing habits in schools. When collective efficacy is lacking, it affects quality implementation in ways that stifle the spread, depth, sustainability, and ownership of change initiatives. Realizing innovative and lasting changes that become accepted practices and produce positive outcomes is unlikely when efficacy is lacking because efficacy beliefs *affect behavior* in the following ways:

1. A lack of collective efficacy impacts how teams perceive constraints and opportunities afforded in their unique school environments (teams with low efficacy anticipate the futility of their efforts and produce little change).

2. When collective efficacy is reduced, teams show a significant reduction in the goals they set, and this impacts motivational investments.

3. Collective efficacy beliefs shape experiences (low expectations become self-fulfilling prophecies).

> *When collective efficacy is lacking, it affects behavior in ways that stifle the spread, depth, sustainability, and ownership of change initiatives.*

We will expand on how a lack of collective efficacy stifles change in each of these ways in the section that follows.

Whatever We Do Isn't Going to Matter

A middle school housed a junior community living program that was designed to meet the needs of students in fourth through sixth grades with severe learning and physical disabilities. Most students attending the program were bussed in from other areas because the schools in their local neighborhoods did not have the facilities required to serve their needs. All of the students had either limited mobility or limited speech or a combination of the two. In a self-contained classroom, the students were provided with modified programs in which the long-term aim was to help them integrate into communities with some degree of independence. Most students' immediate learning needs were largely centered around effective communication and self-advocacy skills.

The administrators at this school were well aware of the evidence that demonstrated the benefits of including students with special education needs in all aspects of school life. Some benefits included an increased sense of belonging, the opportunity to see how different people interact, and a better appreciation for understanding individual differences. In an effort to provide inclusion opportunities for the students in the junior community living program, the administrators began approaching the entire faculty and shared ideas and strategies for integrating students into art, music, and physical education classes as a starting point. They knew that the mainstream classroom teachers would need help differentiating their instruction, and they offered to provide support, additional resources, and release time for teachers to engage in professional learning.

Unfortunately, the administrators met with much resistance from the junior grade teaching team, and this issue became an ongoing challenge in their leadership practice. Teachers were reluctant to provide instruction for the students in the community living program and complained that they should not be required to when a modified program already existed at the school. Regardless, the principals scheduled times during the week for teaching assistants to accompany the students from the community living program into various classes. Then the art, music, and physical education teachers started rearranging their schedules, at the last minute on these days, in a way that made integration more difficult and less appropriate. For example, the teacher who was teaching art extended her mathematics lessons so that her art classes were shorter and less frequently offered. The music teacher used the time when students from the community living program were to be included in her class as testing periods, and as a result, very little music instruction took place during these classes. The physical education teacher often had the students from the community living program observing from the sidelines rather than participating in the physical activities he had designed for his students.

When talking with the teachers, it became clear to the principal that teachers' beliefs were a major barrier to integrating students with special education needs into their classes. The teachers did not believe that they could make any significant gains given the special education needs of the students and that any additional effort they put forth would not result in students acquiring the knowledge and skills in their subject area. As one teacher bluntly (and mistakenly) put it, "Whatever we do isn't going to matter."

In the preceding examples, teachers' beliefs held them back from doing the work to figure out how to make inclusion work in their contexts; in fact, they went the other way and actively (or passively) resisted! The evidence-based promise of inclusion was not realized in practice because the junior grade teachers' lack of efficacy caused them to think that their efforts were pointless. Believing their efforts would not amount to much caused teachers to put up barriers that hindered the spread of inclusion in this one middle school.

> *"Efficacy beliefs influence how people feel, think, motivate themselves, and behave"* (Bandura, 1993, p. 118).

Collective Efficacy's Role in Team Motivation

A second way in which efficacy beliefs can pose a major barrier to quality implementation is through motivational processes. In the 1960s, psychologist Edwin Locke developed the goal-setting theory of motivation (Locke & Latham, 2006). The theory states that goal setting is linked to task performance. When teams set challenging goals and receive appropriate feedback, it contributes to better task performance. In other words, goals provide direction to educators (and students) about what needs to be done and how much effort is required to succeed. As long as the goal is not too far out of reach, challenging goals raise motivation for success.

According to Locke and Latham (2002), goal setting improves performance in the following four ways. Goals direct attention to the task at hand, keeping teams focused on what they are trying to accomplish. Second, goals mobilize efforts, and teams work harder as a result of having goals. Third, when teams have a specific goal, they are more likely to persist and less likely to give up easily. Finally, goals promote the development of improved strategies. When teams recognize that their current actions are not helping them progress toward their goals, they devise better strategies to get them there. In other words, goals are important in creating the conditions for the productive patterns of behavior that we associate with quality implementation—that is, getting a critical mass of people to apply and experiment with *what's supposed to work,* assessing impact relative to the intended outcomes, learning about what worked and what didn't work and why within respective contexts, and then making the necessary modifications based on feedback. We will explore more about goal setting later in this book. For now, it is important to understand the relationship between goal setting and collective efficacy.

The stronger a team's beliefs in its collective capability, the higher the goals a team sets for itself (Bandura, 1998). When collective efficacy decreases, however, teams show a significant reduction in goal setting and attainment. An experiment, in which the real intention of the study was kept a secret from participants, helps us in understanding this relationship further. The following depiction of this "masked experiment" demonstrates how diminishing collective efficacy results in reduced goals and decreased effort.

Diminished Collective Efficacy
Results in a Reduction of Goals and Effort

To better understand how collective efficacy impacts team goals and commitment, researchers Greenlees, Graydon, and Maynard (2000) set up an experiment that involved feedback manipulation. Participants were unaware of the true nature of the study and were recruited through an advertisement that described a team cycling competition. People thought they signed up for a race in which the task was to obtain the fastest combined team time on stationary bikes, riding a distance of two thousand meters. What the researchers were really interested in finding out was how collective efficacy impacted goal selection and effort.

Participants were assigned to triads and told that they were competing against one hundred other teams. In fact, only twenty-six triads existed: thirteen triads randomly assigned to a "high-efficacy group" and thirteen assigned to a "low-efficacy group." Teams agreed to compete in two time trials, and before each time trial, the cyclers were asked to set (a) a time goal and (b) a finishing-place goal (out of one hundred teams) that they felt their team could achieve in the forthcoming time trial.

> Cyclists were also told that prizes would be determined based on points gained over two time trials and that points were awarded for time taken, finishing position, and the team's ability to achieve both the time goal and the finishing-place goal. Furthermore, participants believed not just that more points would be awarded for the achievement of higher goals but also that a penalty of twenty-five points would be incurred for each goal that was not achieved (this was to ensure that teams set realistic goals rather than excessively high ones). To help cyclers decide on their team's time goals, they were told that the range of times that had been recorded for the task in the past had been between thirty and ninety seconds.

Both groups received bogus feedback in between the first time trial and the second. Those in the high-efficacy group were told that their team had completed the course within a range of thirty to forty seconds and that they were currently in the top 5 percent of teams in the competition. Those in the low-efficacy group were told that their team had completed the two thousand meters in excess of forty-five seconds and that they were in the bottom 20 percent of teams.

Greenlees and colleagues hypothesized that the low-efficacy group would select a less difficult goal in between time trials. The researchers were also interested to find out if collective efficacy impacted choice of activity and hypothesized that individuals in the high-efficacy group would express a preference for more challenging group activities than those in the low-efficacy group. Finally, the researchers predicted that a reduction in collective efficacy would result in poorer performance.

The results indicated that after manipulating a team's belief in their combined ability through bogus performance feedback, collective efficacy did influence goal selection. Individuals in the low-efficacy feedback group selected less difficult time goals and less difficult finishing-place goals in the second timed trial than they had in the first. They also found that an individual's belief in his or her group contributed to his or her decision to participate in particular future activities. Those in the low-efficacy feedback group selected a lower standard of activity than did those in the high-efficacy group. Finally, the experiment also revealed that those in the low-efficacy condition took longer to complete the task after receiving bogus feedback. They slackened their efforts while those in the high-efficacy group maintained their efforts.

Collective efficacy is one important factor that teams tap into when determining goals that they eventually adopt as shown in the experiment above. When collective efficacy is reduced, teams show a significant reduction in the goals they set. Goals influence team performance through motivational processes, and when efficacy is reduced, it can become a barrier to implementation because it results in less challenging goals; lower standards; and, ultimately, a decrease in effort.

> When collective efficacy is reduced, teams show a significant reduction in the goals they set.

In schools, the motivational impact of goals is jeopardized by a lack of collective efficacy. When goals are not accomplished, it can lead to frustration and lower motivation. If a faculty's sense of collective efficacy becomes diminished, it is likely that it will show a reduction in goal selection. As noted earlier, challenging goals lead to greater effort and increased persistence. They also help teams to develop strategies when their current practices are not resulting in the outcomes intended. Since the most effective performance results when goals are specific and challenging (Locke & Latham, 2006), diminished efficacy will ultimately impact quality implementation. Innovative and lasting change will be thwarted because lower goals result in reduced effort and a lack of persistence; therefore, improvement strategies are unlikely to reach depth, sustainability, spread, and shift in reform ownership.

> In schools, the motivational impact of goals is jeopardized by a lack of collective efficacy.

Collective Efficacy Beliefs Shape Experience

A third way in which efficacy beliefs hinder quality implementation occurs because efficacy beliefs shape experiences. A team's perceived experience is their reality. Low expectations become self-fulfilling prophecies in a cycle of learned helplessness. The Golem effect is a psychological phenomenon in which low expectations lead to poor performance. When teams believe that they won't do well, they don't. When teacher teams hold low expectations, they produce behaviors that negatively impact the performance of their students while the students themselves produce negative behaviors (Brophy, 1983). Educators' beliefs influence their actions toward their classes, which in turn impact students' beliefs about their own abilities. Low expectations for success become barriers for both teacher teams and students because regardless of their accuracy, they become self-fulfilling prophecies.

The effects of expectations occur not only in classrooms but in laboratories, hospitals, sports, management, and the military as well. Sometimes lower expectations are placed upon teams by supervisors or by the teams themselves. An example of how low expectations produce negative or minimal outcomes in teams can be seen in the Metropolitan Life Insurance experiment (Livingston, 2003).

An experiment that played out over the course of three years demonstrated that the Golem effect is just as prevalent in office buildings as it is in schools. In many studies of the Golem effect, individuals are the unit of analysis, but the Metropolitan Life Insurance experiment (Livingston, 2003) demonstrated that self-fulfilling prophecies play out when teams are the unit of analysis as well. In the 1960s, a district manager at the Metropolitan Life Insurance Company observed that top-performing insurance agencies grew faster than poorer performing agencies and decided to reconfigure teams to try to capitalize on gains produced by high-performing teams. Individuals were placed on one of three teams depending on what was expected of their performance. The best managers were assigned to teams that comprised the most superior insurance agents. These teams were referred to as the "super-staff." Agents who were expected to produce at lower levels were grouped together with the least able managers. Finally, those deemed average employees composed teams with average managers assigned to lead them.

After the first quarter, the super-staff team exceeded expectations, and the overall agency performance improved by 40 percent in the first year. As the company expanded, the experiment continued into a second year, and production and profits continued to grow. Even though the performance in the overall agency grew, production declined for those assigned to the lower units. In an attempt to avoid situations that might have led to failure (and additional damage to their egos) employees assigned to this unit made fewer sales calls. By the end of the third year, only one employee remained. The theory of the Golem effect became a realization for those labeled as lower performers at the Metropolitan Life Insurance Company.

What makes this experiment even more interesting, however, is what happened with the average teams. The productivity of the average teams increased significantly and by *a higher percentage* than that of the super-staff teams even though the district manager expected only average performance. To help explain why, we can look to the assistant manager who was leading the average team.

She refused to believe that she was less capable than the manager in charge of the high-performing group or that the insurance agents in the super-staff group had greater ability than the agents on her team. High expectations were reflected in her conversations with her team and her actions toward them. As a result, she inspired greater productivity.

One final interesting note concerns a manager in another district in the Metropolitan Life Insurance Company's corporation who also established superior, average, and low units even though he was convinced that he had no outstanding agents. He was quoted as saying, "All of my assistant managers and agents are either average or incompetent" (Livingstone, 2003, Impact on Productivity section). Although he hoped to duplicate the results from the neighboring district, the agents in his area were aware of his low expectations; therefore his experiment failed.

This example helps to shed light on why ability grouping in schools has very little influence on student achievement. Ability grouping is when students are assigned to classes on the basis of ability, also known as streaming or tracking. Hattie (2009) noted,

> Empirical evidence leads to a conclusion that there is a close to zero effect from tracking, but the qualitative literature indicates that there may be quite different teaching and interactions in the low versus high tracked classes. The qualitative evidence indicates that low tracked classes are more fragmented, less engaging, and taught by fewer well-trained teachers. (p. 91)

As we saw in the experiment above, individuals and teams are well aware of the expectations that are set upon them. Whether it is teachers' expectations of students or administrators' expectations of teachers, the individuals and groups know who among them are considered the super-staff and who are not. Expectations are reflected in conversations and can be inferred from the tasks that teams are assigned. In schools, it might sound like this: "Our primary teachers are an incredible team! They have what it takes to make a difference." Of course, the inference here is that other divisions do not constitute effective teams and do not have what it takes!

Lack of efficacy is tantamount to holding low expectations. Both affect behavior in ways that stifle quality implementation because as noted earlier, beliefs shape experiences. Self-fulfilling prophecies result in cycles of learned helplessness in which low efficacy results in low effort, which results in low performance and so on. The Golem effect impacts the level of effort the team expends. Quality implementation requires effort as teams try to make evidence-based practices work in context. Eventually, members who believe they are part of an ineffective team accept the validity of the label they are

Lindsley, Brass, and Thomas (1995) noted that once a group is labeled (or labels itself) as bad, it tends to initiate a self-fulfilling prophecy whereby, regardless of its performance, the group's beliefs generate a reality that confirms its expectations.

assigned (in some cases, the label they assign to themselves) and stop trying. Quality implementation cannot be realized in a culture where there are pockets of low expectations because of the critical mass needed to do the work necessary to achieve innovative and lasting change. As we saw in the Metropolitan Life Insurance experiment, teams will want to avoid situations that may lead to disappointments (and additional damage to their egos), so they will be less likely to experiment, assess the outcomes of new strategies and approaches in their practice, and use feedback to make necessary adjustments.

In Conclusion

What we examined in this chapter were the implications for quality implementation when efficacy is lacking. Diminished collective efficacy becomes a significant barrier to quality implementation because it affects behavior in three ways. The first is related to how teams perceive constraints and opportunities in their unique contexts. Faulty perceptions cause teams to anticipate efforts as pointless; therefore they do not even try. The second was related to how motivation is affected through goal setting. When efficacy is lacking, teams reduce their goals and their efforts—as demonstrated in the triad cycling experiment. Finally, a lack of efficacy shapes experience through self-fulfilling prophecies. The Golem effect causes resignation and improvement efforts are easily abandoned in order to protect a team's self-esteem as demonstrated in the Metropolitan Life Insurance experiment.

However, we also learned that there is a wealth of research demonstrating that collective efficacy is highly predictive of student achievement, and we argued that it has such a high effect size because it enables quality implementation. Just as a diminished sense of efficacy is a barrier to quality implementation because it effects behavior that undermines change, a heightened sense of efficacy effects behavior that supports change. The fact that collective efficacy becomes manifested in educators' practices accounts for the reason why it works. It influences student achievement indirectly through a constellation of productive patterns of behavior on the part of the adults in the building. A faculty's combined belief in its ability to positively influence student achievement, over and above any other factor, results in depth, spread, sustainability, and ownership of change initiatives. When collective efficacy is strong, evidence-based promises of improvement-oriented interventions get realized. We explore how a heightened sense of collective efficacy affects behaviors in ways that support quality implementation in the chapter that follows.

TIME FOR REFLECTION

1. Given your context, what are some potential negative consequences of a diminished sense of collective efficacy?

2. What faulty perceptions have surfaced in your work related to school improvement?

3. Have you seen the Golem effect at work? If so, what steps might your team begin to take to change this?

COLLECTIVE EFFICACY AS AN ENABLER OF QUALITY IMPLEMENTATION

Thus far, we have argued that evidence-based practices can achieve their promise only when they are subject to a recursive professional learning methodology (which we refer to as progressive inquiry) whereby they are made to work in specific contexts. This is a process that we have defined as quality implementation and, as we saw in Chapter 2, without the right beliefs, the "work" of quality implementation will not unfold and evidence of scaled change will remain elusive. We saw how diminished collective efficacy was a barrier to quality implementation because it negatively impacted how teams perceived constraints, set goals, expended effort toward goals, and negatively shaped experiences. In this chapter, we assume an appreciative stance and explore how enhanced collective efficacy enables quality implementation by positively impacting how teams perceive opportunities (rather than constraints) given their unique environments, set goals, expend effort toward goals, and shape experiences in positive ways.

Integrating Daily Physical Activity in Elementary Schools

In order to promote healthy lifestyles by increasing children's activity levels, the National Association for Sports and Physical Education recommends that children participate in sixty minutes of physical activity daily. This recommendation had implications for school reforms in many U.S. states and Canadian provinces. Educators were called upon to make a serious commitment to increasing school children's daily physical activity to improve children's health. Since the recommendation was beyond the scope of what could be delivered in physical education classes, change initiatives called for implementation of physical activity into subject areas in addition to physical education. Some classroom teachers stepped up and took on the responsibility, while many did not. Even though ten to fifteen minutes of daily physical activity became a policy in many school districts, the quality of implementation varied.

In 2007, Parks and colleagues set out to discover the role of collective efficacy in empowering teachers to increase children's physical activity in classrooms by conducting research in forty-four elementary schools (Parks, Solmon, & Lee, 2007). Three hundred and fourteen teachers and thirty-eight administrators took part in the study. Findings suggested that educators' willingness to integrate daily physical activity *was* related to individual and collective efficacy. In schools with high individual and collective efficacy, teachers tended to report that they were willing to integrate daily physical activity in their classrooms.

> *Willingness to integrate daily physical activity was related to individual and collective efficacy.*

This study provides insights into how to reach quality implementation of evidence-based strategies, such as integrating physical activity into the classroom, through a collective efficacy lens. Two factors in this study predicted both individual and collective efficacy: mastery experiences and the institutional environment. Mastery experiences (also known as performance accomplishments) generate an influential source of efficacy because repeated successes raise future expectations for success (Bandura, 1998). Of the successes teachers experienced in implementing daily physical activity in their classrooms, most influentially predicted the strength of educators' individual efficacy. We will discuss more about mastery experiences and other sources of efficacy in the next chapter. For now, note that both mastery experiences and the institutional environment predicted efficacy. More importantly, the institutional environment was the strongest predictor of *collective efficacy*. In schools where the faculty believed in the importance of movement for students' well-being and academic achievement and valued movement as an important strategy to attain

> *The institutional environment was the strongest predictor of collective efficacy.*

their goals, collective efficacy was higher. This finding reinforces an argument we set forth earlier. Collective efficacy can advance only by addressing the contextual factors in the unique school environments in which efficacy beliefs are formed.

How Collective Efficacy Drives Quality Implementation

Collective efficacy *drives the right kinds of behaviors* that are instrumental to quality implementation. These include engagement in what we have referred to as professional learning structures that reflect a progressive inquiry methodology that results in focused effort, persistence, application, experimentation, and analysis in search of a better way of doing things in schools and classrooms.

Efficacious teams do not just welcome new instructional practices into the mix. They also engage in progressive inquiry: setting and monitoring common goals, focusing their combined efforts, using feedback to adjust their next steps—all while recognizing that innovative and lasting change requires some discomfort. They tolerate that discomfort. And they work interdependently to take control, motivationally invest, and shape experiences based on high expectations.

Collective efficacy drives behaviors that produce quality implementation because efficacy beliefs affect behavior in the following three ways:

1. When collective efficacy is present, teams figure out ways to exercise some control, even in environments containing few opportunities and many constraints.

2. Collective efficacy results in motivational investments.

3. Collective efficacy beliefs shape experience in positive ways through self-fulfilling prophecies.

We will expand on how collective efficacy beliefs effect behavior that advances change in each of these ways in the section that follows.

How Teams Exercise Control

A predominant perception in some schools is that educators are limited in the influence they can have on students who live in poverty. When students come from low socioeconomic backgrounds, educators sometimes falsely assume they are less capable of academic achievement. Some educators view student poverty as a limiting constraint, and when educators attribute low student performance to demographic variables, little change is produced because educators do not believe their efforts will amount to much.

However, *regardless of student demographics* some schools are more effective and more equitable than others. Why do some schools experience greater results when compared to others who serve students with similar backgrounds, race, and socioeconomic status? Researchers investigated this topic in two recent research studies. Both studies involved schools serving economically disadvantaged students, and even though the studies took place in different countries, and at different times, and were conducted by different researchers, the investigators reached similar conclusions. Teachers' beliefs directly predicted students' academic experiences in the successful schools regardless of student background characteristics.

Teachers' beliefs directly predicted students' academic experiences in the successful schools regardless of student background characteristics.

In Texas, as in many other U.S. states and Canadian provinces, certain agencies responsible for public education exist. The Texas Education Agency rates school campuses based on student testing and accountability measures. Schools receive ratings from "superior" to "substandard." Throughout the state in areas with low socio-economic status, some schools were excelling, while others were failing to meet minimum standards based on the ratings from the Texas Education Agency. In common, the schools all qualified as serving economically disadvantaged students. Drawing on a random sample of schools that failed to meet the minimum standard and schools that excelled in all areas for two consecutive years, the researchers conducted group comparison research to determine the level of relationship between collective teacher efficacy and student achievement.

The collective efficacy of teachers from the superior campuses was *significantly higher* than that of the teachers from the academically unacceptable campuses. Sandoval, Challoo, and Kupczynski (2011) found that efficacious schools were able to impact student achievement because teachers believed in their own and their colleagues' ability to enhance student learning regardless of the students' home environment and socioeconomic status. The researchers noted that resilience of the faculties' shared vision for the success of their students "assisted them in overcoming the socioeconomic barriers that prevent so many other school campuses from obtaining exemplary ratings" (p. 19).

A year later, a similar study was carried out in Canada. Focusing on thirty-three secondary schools serving disadvantaged communities in Quebec, Archambault, Janosz, and Chouinard (2012) explored the effect of teacher efficacy on student outcomes and noted that variations existed between classrooms. Why is it that in some classes, students achieve better outcomes than others?

"Teachers in schools with high collective efficacy do not accept low student achievement as an inevitable by-product of low socioeconomic status, lack of ability, or family background. They roll up their sleeves and get the job done" (Tschannen-Moran & Barr, 2004, p. 192).

In this study, teachers' beliefs played a *larger role* in predicting student outcomes than students' prior achievement and/or socioeconomic status. The more efficacious educators felt in helping students succeed, the more student achievement increased over the year. The researchers concluded that teachers' collective efficacy beliefs can promote low-socioeconomic-status students' academic achievement.

As noted above, collective efficacy impacts how educators perceive constraints and opportunities in schools. If educators view students' socioeconomic status or family backgrounds as limiting (or special education needs as evidenced in the previous chapter), they perceive their efforts as pointless and are less inclined to take action. When teams believe their efforts will not amount to much, they do not go that "extra mile." However, when collective efficacy is established, teams figure out ways to exercise some control, as demonstrated in the studies above. This shows one of the ways in which efficacy beliefs drive the right kinds of behavior that prove instrumental to quality implementation. Educators do not let constraints get in the way. They rally to get a critical mass, doing the right thing, for the right reason, at the right time, while assessing the impact of their actions. By engaging in progressive inquiry, they find ways to bring theory and practice together in their unique contexts in order to produce positive outcomes for students—regardless of other circumstances. They go outside their comfort zones; use focused, goal-driven activity to improve an area of weakness; and make changes based on feedback.

Progressive Inquiry Methodologies Include These Tactics:

- Monitoring and discussing activities or projects to learn from successful and from failed initiatives

- Engaging in systematic analysis of data

- Regularly drawing on research and/or outside expertise to improve practice

- Initiating intentional professional learning opportunities in relation to inquiry

- Regularly challenging one another's assumptions about teaching and learning

- Being receptive to feedback on teaching from school colleagues

- Talking openly with school colleagues about differing views, opinions, and values

- Dealing openly with professional conflicts that arise in school

---

Source: Katz, Earl, and Ben Jaafar (2009), p. 73.

Motivational Investments

A second way in which efficacy beliefs support quality implementation is through motivational investments. As we saw in the previous chapter, goal setting links to task performance through motivational investments. Teams anticipate and form beliefs about what they can accomplish together. They set goals and make plans in order to realize desired outcomes. In the example shared next, we will see how collective efficacy results in motivational investments through goal setting.

We interviewed Stacy Allison, the first American woman to reach the top of Mount Everest; the highest mountain on Earth, Everest's elevation measures over 29,000 feet. This feat cannot be accomplished alone. Everest climbers face many dangers including altitude sickness, potential hazards from wind and snow, and avalanches. Many people have died trying to make it to the top. In our interview with Allison, she noted that only 25 percent of climbers have a chance of succeeding and that success requires an enormous amount of teamwork and cooperation—not only for success but for survival too.

In her first attempt, Allison and her team were caught in the worst storm to hit the mountain in forty years. Hundred mile-an-hour winds and avalanches surrounded them. As a result, they were trapped in a snow cave for five days where they had to make the best use of their resources, dig out the opening to the cave every fifteen to twenty minutes in order to have enough oxygen to breathe, and think very strategically about their next moves. After the storm blew over, the team continued up the mountain where they reached their next camp at 25,000 feet. Here, they were holed up for another three days, and because of their deteriorating health, they had to turn back.

Allison told us that she was unsuccessful in her first attempt, in part, due to the storm but also because she put her personal goals ahead of the team, wanting to be the first person to reach the summit at all costs. Learning from her failure, Allison noted that she reflected on what she needed to do as a team member the next time so that the team could succeed. "When we help other people succeed, we in turn succeed ourselves," said Allison (S. Allison, personal interview, January 27, 2018).

Allison described other important lessons she learned during her second attempt and successful climb to the summit. Allison recollected that when crossing the Khumbu glacier, in the changing environment, it was the team members (not the leader) who were accountable for each other's safety; therefore, the team made the decisions together. Some decisions had to be made in the face of uncertainty, and the team had to be ready to adapt their route in an instant in response to the shifting ice and snow. She noted that when climbing shoulder to shoulder along the mountain, it was really important to ensure that the team felt connected with each other and that they felt they were part of something special.

While being first to navigate a series of aluminum ladders that had been linked together and propped across a seventy-five-foot-deep crevasse as a makeshift bridge, Allison noted the importance of showing confidence to her teammates who had to follow her lead. She advised that when working with teams, it is important to ensure that doubt does not become the team's biggest leech (leeches were literally attached to Stacy's body at one point during the climb). She also placed trust in her teammates' competency in performing their jobs. She had not checked any of the anchors that were put in place to secure and steady the ladders, but she trusted her teammates who had taken on that responsibility. Allison told us that after twenty-nine days on the mountain, she made it to the top and credits teamwork and collective efficacy in her accomplishment.

Allison's story helps to illustrate how efficacy beliefs come to fruition. One can only imagine the numerous obstacles that Stacy and her team faced during the journey to the top and the persistence, commitment, and effort that were necessary to succeed. The team needed to ensure the best use of their resources because their lives depended upon it. Even though Allison did not succeed in her first attempt, she did not let that discourage her from trying again. Her team had a great deal of collective efficacy because they placed confidence in each other, believed that together they could conquer Everest, and did not let vulnerability deter them when faced with extreme challenges along the way.

As we have seen, efficacy beliefs play a central role in motivational investments (Bandura, 1998). Goals and attributions are two forms of motivators in which theories about motivation and performance have been built. Ways in which collective efficacy results in motivational investments through goals and attributions are shared in the section that follows.

How Goal Setting Influences Motivation

The collective efficacy of Allison's team played a central role in determining their goals and motivating their behavior. As we learned in the previous chapter, goals provide direction about what needs to be done and how much effort is required in order to succeed. The goals teams choose to pursue are based partially on their collective efficacy beliefs. Greenlees and colleagues' (2000) bogus cycling competition described in the previous chapter demonstrated how when collective efficacy is reduced, teams show a significant reduction in their goal selection. We also know that the stronger the collective efficacy, the higher the goals teams set for themselves.

In the successful Mount Everest climb, Stacy Allison spoke to the role that goal setting played in motivating her team. She told us that during the twenty-nine days on the mountain, the team would often grow tired and at times felt they did not have the strength to continue on. However, when the team experienced difficulties, felt exhausted, or did not have the strength to take another step, they could look up at the peak of the mountain and be reminded of their goal. When looking up at the summit and realizing that they wanted to be there, the team was motivated to continue. Allison also pointed out the beauty of climbing a mountain: You can actually see your goal, and she noted the importance of educators *visualizing* goals that aren't right there in front of them. Readers will recall that challenging goals raise motivation for success (Locke & Latham, 2006). Motivation for success creates opportunities in which innovative and lasting change can be realized.

> It is partly on the basis of efficacy beliefs that teams choose what goal challenges to undertake, how much effort to invest, and how long to persist when faced with difficulties (Bandura, 1997).

How Causal Attributions
Influence Motivation

Collective efficacy results in motivational investments through causal attributions as well.

Teams' successes and failures impact collective efficacy. How much it is impacted and in which direction varies depending on if the team attributes performance to factors that are within their control or factors that are uncontrollable. When teams share a sense of collective efficacy they attribute failure to insufficient effort, inadequate strategies, or unfavorable circumstances (Bandura, 1998). Failure produces a reduction in efficacy when attributed to inability (Bandura, 1977). In the first attempt to climb Mount Everest, Allison attributed failure to the unfavorable circumstances (the harsh weather conditions). Attributing the failure to the storm that hit the mountain and not to the team's ability helped in maintaining a high sense of efficacy, which translated into the motivation to try again.

The Pygmalion Effect

A third way in which efficacy beliefs drive the right kinds of behavior that support quality implementation is through self-fulfilling prophecies. In Chapter 2, we saw how low expectations perpetuated the conditions that led to underperformance for teams in the Metropolitan Life Insurance Company. Just as the effects of low expectations result in self-fulfilling prophecies, high expectations stemming from a shared sense of efficacy become self-fulfilling prophecies as well.

High expectations refer to holding all students to high standards and providing appropriately challenging material. It is the belief that students are capable of comprehending complex text, solving difficult problems, and developing a high degree of skill across disciplines. High expectations perpetuate the conditions that lead to higher performance in schools because teachers' expectations affect students' expectations of their performance and their motivation.

High expectations stemming from a shared sense of efficacy become self-fulfilling prophecies.

The effects that high expectations can have on performance, commonly known as the Pygmalion effect, have been well researched and documented in schools. Rosenthal and Jacobson (1968) were the first to study and document the effects that teacher expectations have on student performance. More recently, Boser, Wilhelm, and Hanna (2014) found that when high school teachers hold higher expectations, students are far more likely to graduate from college. The researchers noted, "All else equal, 10th grade students who had teachers with higher expectations were more than three times more likely to graduate from college than students who had teachers with lower expectations" (p. 2). Other researchers have found that teachers' expectations of preschoolers show a robust prediction of high school grade-point average (Alvidrez & Weinstein, 1999). Numerous studies document the Pygmalion effect in other contexts as well, including the military, management, and sports teams.

Students are well aware of teachers' expectations. They know who are the low achievers and the high achievers in their classes— even at a very young age. They are also aware of the differential treatment of themselves and others in the classroom. Students recognize that lower achievers receive more negative feedback, less freedom and choice, and stricter adherence to the rules.

The Pygmalion effect is key to quality implementation because it evokes positive behaviors in both educators and students alike. When teachers believe students can achieve, they put forth greater effort, provide additional support, and behave in other ways that positively influence students' beliefs about themselves. Students internalize positive labels and identities and, therefore, behave in ways that increase their own chances of success.

In Conclusion

Understanding how collective efficacy regulates behavior is important if teams aspire to create the conditions for change in their schools. Collective efficacy is the link between effort and results. When collective efficacy is present, the process through which evidence-based promises of improvement-oriented interventions get realized in practice is strengthened. Efficacious teams hold a strong conviction that they can succeed despite all other circumstances. The confidence they place in their team's ability results in sustained effort and perseverance. They mobilize their resources and rely on their training in order to execute the skills necessary to achieve significant positive results. Regardless of the challenge, they band together and get the job done.

Collective efficacy results in more productive behaviors including the implementation of evidence-based approaches. Educators' productive behaviors, established through their collective efficacy, help to produce measurable gains in student success, regardless of students' low socioeconomic status. The professional practices of educators and the way their schools operate can overcome the effects of poverty. In the next chapter, we'll explore the sources of collective efficacy beliefs and continue to consider how to achieve quality implementation through a collective efficacy framework.

TIME FOR REFLECTION ————————————————

1. What are the attributes of an efficacious team?

2. What are some strengths your team currently possesses?

3. What is the relationship between teamwork and results?

FOSTERING BELIEFS TO REALIZE QUALITY IMPLEMENTATION

CHAPTER 4

CREATING MASTERY MOMENTS

So far, we have seen how educators' beliefs affect thought patterns in ways that either support or impede quality implementation. Teams who lack collective efficacy are preoccupied by constraints, show significant reduction in the goals they set, and lower their efforts. A lack of collective efficacy also results in self-fulfilling prophecies in which cycles of learned helplessness shape teams' experiences in negative ways. On the other hand, teams who hold strong beliefs in their combined ability figure out ways to exercise control over the challenges that surround them. Efficacious groups exert greater effort. Teams muster up the strength, motivation, and resolve needed to meet challenging goals. Finally, just as the effects of low expectations result in self-fulfilling prophecies, high expectations stemming from a shared sense of efficacy become self-fulfilling prophecies leading to greater achievements.

> Educators' beliefs affect thought patterns in ways that either support or impede quality implementation.

When collective efficacy is firmly established, teams persist through the discomfort felt when trying to put into practice something they have not tried before. Through engaging in progressive inquiry, efficacious teams apply evidence-based strategies, experiment with making them work in their context, and monitor progress toward their goals in order to adjust their course based on feedback. In this sense, collective efficacy drives the right kinds of behaviors, those instrumental to quality implementation.

A firm sense of collective efficacy contributes significantly to successful school improvement through quality implementation. It is therefore important to understand how teams form beliefs about what they are able to and unable to accomplish. Four different sources provide teams with information about their capability for dealing with challenging circumstances (Bandura, 1977). Collective efficacy beliefs form based on information obtained from mastery experiences, vicarious experiences, social persuasion, and affective states. It is important to understand not only how teams form beliefs about their combined capability but also how teams capitalize on the sources of collective efficacy as a way to achieve quality implementation. In the second half of this book, we take a closer look at the sources of collective efficacy and identify what school teams can do to strengthen efficacy-shaping sources. We will also share structures that reflect a progressive inquiry methodology and thus support quality implementation.

In this chapter, we examine the strongest source of collective efficacy, mastery experiences, by providing examples and describing key features of mastery environments. We also consider implications for practice and make suggestions about what teams can focus on in order to tap into mastery experiences as a source of collective efficacy.

Mastery Experiences

Repeated successful performances (mastery moments) constitute the most significant source of collective efficacy because they draw on firsthand experiences (Bandura, 1977). When teams set out to accomplish a task and achieve success based on sustained efforts, it raises mastery expectations. Teams come to believe that through their combined efforts they can accomplish their goals. Teams raise their expectations for future success because they experienced success in the past.

Once teachers gain evidence of improvements in student learning that result from changes in teaching, a significant change in teachers' attitudes and beliefs occurs (Guskey, 2000). The experience of quality implementation caused the change in these teachers' beliefs. The process is actually more cyclical than linear. Changes in beliefs lead to additional changes in practice that result in greater increases in student achievement, which positively influences beliefs, and so on. As student results continued to increase, so did the faculty's collective efficacy.

A Case of Successful School Improvement Teams

In Chapter 3, we presented research that demonstrated how mastery experiences and the institutional environment predicted collective efficacy in elementary schools in relation to integrating daily physical activity into classrooms. We also witnessed, firsthand, how impactful collaborative experiences define moments as efficacy-strengthening sources. One specific example took place in a high school in Ontario, Canada, where teams of teachers worked interdependently to improve students' overall experiences and achievement. Five teams, led by teacher leaders, focused on priorities related to the school's improvement goals. As a professional learning community, they voluntarily observed each other's practice (see observation as an efficacy-strengthening vicarious experience in Chapter 5) in an effort to increase the use of explicit learning intentions and success criteria, which were key evidence-based practices recently introduced in the school district. They explored different strategies for providing effective feedback to students as part of their daily instruction. In addition, they spent extra hours working with students who had been identified as needing additional time and support in the areas of literacy and mathematics.

In retelling the experience, the teachers recalled not only their awareness of the day when results from the provincial standardized test would be released but also waiting in anticipation to see if their efforts had paid off. They had provided practice tests and individual feedback, based on their assessment of the practice test, to every student prior to the actual administration of the official test. That spring, the school's results showed a 21 percent increase in the success rate for first-time eligible students and a 19 percent increase in the success rate for previously eligible students. In addition, the gap in achievement between students enrolled in applied courses (workplace pathway) and students enrolled in academic courses (university pathway) decreased by 21 percent. The results proved not only confirming to teachers but also eye-opening as they realized how their efforts resulted in measurable increases for students in their school.

> *The results proved not only confirming to teachers but also eye-opening as they realized how their efforts resulted in measurable increases for students in their school.*

The team's quality implementation experience resulted in further refinements to their practice. Realization of innovative and lasting changes occurred when what was working began to spread throughout the school. Teachers understood the strategies they were using with greater depth and therefore used them with greater effectiveness. And teachers felt empowered, gaining a sense of voice and agency in school improvement efforts. The things they were doing as teachers made the difference. When teachers got better, students got better.

Not only do mastery experiences influence beliefs regarding a group's combined ability in schools and classrooms, but they are also the most potent source of collective efficacy in other domains. Research has demonstrated that mastery experiences (gaining information relevant to progressing at work) act as an effective work recovery strategy, moderating the effects between occupational stress and mental health symptoms among firefighters (Sawhney, Jennings, Britt, & Sliter, 2017).

Goddard (2001) conducted research to test the assumption that mastery experiences influence teachers' collective efficacy. In the forty-seven schools included in the study, collective efficacy varied considerably. Upon examining which school-level factors could predict between-school variability in collective efficacy, Goddard found that neither socioeconomic status nor race were statistically significant in regard to the differences among schools. Mastery experiences *alone* independently explained the variation in collective efficacy.

Clearly, mastery experiences hold a lot of weight when it comes to building confidence and motivating team efforts. Drawing on four decades of scientific research on human motivation, Pink (2009) identified mastery as one of the three elements of true motivation. He defined mastery as "the desire to get better and better at something that matters" (p. 111). That desire fuels motivational investments and persistent effort. In the example above in the high school in Ontario, getting better at meeting the needs of students, as evidenced by the improved achievement results, led to teachers being highly motivated to continue doing the kinds of things that we defined as indicative of quality implementation.

Other researchers examined the role of mastery experiences in an online weight loss community. Wang and Willis (2016) found that mastery experiences were the most influential source for both dieting and physical activities. Content analysis of online threaded discussions showed that participants celebrated three types of mastery experiences: success with exercise, success with dieting, and success with weight loss. The authors noted another feature of shared experiences among dieters: people posted "not only great achievements but also any small steps toward success no matter how trivial" (p. 661).

Key Features of Mastery Environments

Mastery experiences occur more readily in environments where certain key features are present. These key features include the following: (a) an open-to-learning stance, (b) an orientation toward mastery goals, (c) the engagement of teams in joint work characterized by positive interdependence, and (d) a progress-monitoring system based on success criteria.

In order to gain a better understanding of mastery environments, it is useful to compare and contrast the key features of such environments to those of performance environments (see Figure 2). In performance environments, an emphasis on appearing correct takes the focus away from learning and continuous improvement. These environments are internally competitive, and everyone feels the need to "one-up" each other. The focus on individual performance goals further reinforces internal competition, so rather than working as a collective, teachers work in isolation. Performance is monitored in comparison to how others are doing rather than by a predetermined standard. In the section that follows, we describe each of the key features of mastery environments, which are favorable to fostering efficacy and achieving quality implementation.

There Is an Open-to-Learning Stance

One of us recently had a conversation with a teacher, who is a friend as well. In his fifteenth year as a classroom educator, he feels (and has always felt) no need to engage in professional learning. He said, and was probably so candid because he is a friend, "I know

Sports research demonstrates that the type of environment established by coaches matters in relation to a team's collective efficacy. Studies have examined the relationship between mastery versus performance environments and collective efficacy in sports that require a high degree of interdependence (Cepikkurt & Uluoz, 2017; Kao & Watson, 2014; Magyar, Feltz, & Simpson, 2004). Studies that examined collective efficacy of rowing teams, competitive cheerleading teams, and football teams all concluded that mastery environments were positively related to collective efficacy and that performance environments were negatively related to collective efficacy. Cepikkurt and Uluoz (2017) concluded that the "most important predictor of collective efficacy was a mastery-oriented motivational climate" (p. 95).

Figure 2 Mastery versus Performance Environments

Mastery Environments	Performance Environments
There is an open-to-learning stance.	There is a knowing stance.
There is an orientation toward mastery goals.	There is an orientation toward performance goals.
Teams engage in joint work characterized by positive interdependence.	Teachers work in isolation.
Progress is monitored based on success criteria.	Performance is monitored in relation to how well others are doing.

everything I need to know in order to teach my students." We had to agree to disagree if we were going to remain friends. This *knowing stance* starkly contrasts with what we mean by the term *learning stance*. Teachers' professional learning is integral to school improvement because teacher learning influences classroom practice, an important predictor of student learning and achievement. A key feature of a mastery-oriented environment is that educators have an openness to learning.

Dweck (2008) shared a memory from one of her former professors, whom she described as someone who always told his class to question assumptions. Dweck noted, "There was an assumption," he said, "that schools are for students' learning. Well, why aren't they just as much for teachers' learning?" (p. 195). Dweck recounts this as something she never forgot.

An openness to learning involves openly talking about the challenges that school improvement teams (e.g., teacher or administrator teams) confront in experimenting with different approaches and feedback-seeking behavior. Such an openness to learning characterizes progressive inquiry methodologies. Learning occurs when teams of educators pose questions relevant to their context and based on their students' learning needs; they test and determine solutions, draw conclusions, and make recommendations. In this sense, teams learn by considering not only what is working but also what is not. Mastery cannot be attained in the absence of occasional failures and learning from the team's mistakes. When a learning stance is present, teams learn through trial and error.

> Research shows that "maximum, long-term learning and high performance result when failures are encountered and adjustments are made" (Lindsley, Brass, & Thomas, 1995, p. 650).

On the other hand, when teams adopt a knowing stance, they advocate for the status quo rather than inquire. They are not open to new information that can be used to inform their practice. They simply think (like our friend in the example shared above) that they know everything they need to know. They do not seek feedback or pay attention to any because they see no reason to change strategies or standards. This might be related to their fears of exposing inadequacies or having to acknowledge that perhaps some students may have been better served in the past.

Later in this chapter, we consider how to create the conditions for mastery experiences. One area of focus concerns creating the conditions for teams of educators to learn together. Robinson, Hohepa, and Lloyd's (2009) meta-analysis examined the impact of school leadership on student outcomes and identified promoting and participating in teacher learning and development as the most effective leadership practice with an effect size of 0.84. When leaders have an open-to-learning stance, it can have a significant impact on student outcomes. We will revisit the ideas above and consider implications for practice in moving teams from a knowing stance to a learning stance through cycles of progressive inquiry.

There Is an Orientation Toward Mastery Goals

A second key feature of a mastery environment is a mastery orientation toward goal setting. The work of Carol Dweck, described in her groundbreaking book *Mindset: The New Psychology of Success,* helps us to better understand the differences between mastery goal orientations and performance goal orientations. Dweck (2008) helps us in considering these from a student's perspective. Note the difference between the two goals stated below:

> **Student 1's Goal:** I want to get an A in French.
>
> **Student 2's Goal:** I want to learn the French language.

Student 1's goal represents a performance orientation. Performance approaches suggest that the student's main concern is looking competent in front of others. Performance goals often reflect students who are competitive or seek positive evaluations of ability. Students with performance goal orientations usually want to be seen as smart and want to outperform their classmates because they place value on other people's approval of their performance.

On the other hand, Student 2's goal suggests a mastery orientation where the focus is on the mastery of a task and based on the desire to acquire new knowledge and skills. Mastery goals reflect a student who has an inherent desire to achieve. Students with mastery goal orientations place value on the learning itself. Dweck (2008) noted that mastery goals are associated with more effective strategy use during learning. Students who set mastery-type goals use deeper processing strategies than students who are focused on performance goals. Also, note that Student 1 could get an A in French and still not learn the French language.

Now let us consider the implications of mastery versus performance goal orientations from the perspective of school improvement, team motivation,

> Pink (2009) noted that not all goals are created equal. "Goals that people set for themselves and that are devoted to attaining mastery are usually healthy" (p. 50).

and knowledge and skill acquisition. Note the difference between the two goals stated below:

Team 1's Goal: Attain a 5 percent increase (over last year) on the statewide Grade 6 reading proficiency test.

Team 2's Goal: Ensure all of our students are able to make inferences based on ideas, characters, and events in a variety of texts.

Team 1's goal is an example of a performance-oriented goal. Performance goals do little to intrinsically motivate teams. They often result in pressure on teachers' personal time, stress, and burnout. Team 2's goal is an example of a mastery goal. In schools where key features of mastery environments are present, an orientation toward mastery goals helps to motivate teams in figuring out how to make evidence-based strategies work in their environments. Mastery goals help teams focus on the tasks they need to learn in order to achieve their goals. We will expand more on this later in this chapter, when considering goal-directed behavior as a condition for creating mastery.

> Mastery goals help teams focus on the tasks they need to learn in order to achieve their goals.

Teams Engage in Joint Work Characterized by Positive Interdependence

Joint work is common in mastery environments. We borrow this term from Judith Warren Little's (1990) seminal article in which she called for a harder look at the meaning of collaboration and the circumstances that foster or inhibit it. In distinguishing forms of collegial relations in terms of their demands on autonomy and initiative, Little (1990) noted that distinctions in teachers' collaborations range from sporadic contacts among peers to "joint work of a more rigorous and enduring sort" (p. 513). Joint work involves teachers engaging in "deliberation over difficult and recurring problems of teaching and learning" (p. 520) in service of finding a better way (reflective of progressive inquiry). She expanded upon her explanation of joint work as teachers' collective action and *interdependence* where motivation to participate is based on the fact that each other's contributions are required in order to succeed in independent work.

The firefighting team who saved Kelli Groves and her two daughters (readers will recall the rescue story shared in the preface of this book) were also characterized by a high degree of interdependence. This was also true for Stacy Allison's climbing team and a characteristic of the school improvement work in the high school in Ontario shared at the beginning of this chapter. In 2002, Gully,

Incalcaterra, Joshi, and Beaubein published a meta-analysis demonstrating that the relationship between collective efficacy and team performance is maximized when there is greater positive interdependence among the members of the team. They noted that "when the task and context encourage coordination, communication, and cooperation among members, team-efficacy is related more strongly to performance than when interdependence is low" (Gully et al., 2002, p. 827).

> In 2002, Gully, Incalcaterra, Joshi, and Beaubein published a meta-analysis demonstrating that the relationship between collective efficacy and team performance is maximized when there is greater positive interdependence among the members of the team.

Gully and colleagues (2002) described three types of interdependence: task interdependence, goal interdependence, and outcome interdependence. Task interdependence refers to how connected team members are based on the tasks they are assigned. Some team tasks require very little interdependence, while others require a high degree. Goal interdependence guides efforts based on the implied type of goal (e.g., individual or team). Outcome interdependence refers to the existence of consequences and rewards that are shared by team members and contingent on individual or collective performance.

The Thunder Cape Rescue

Two Canadian Coast Guards, Commanding Officer Sondra Ryersee and Rescue Specialist Jana Lorbetski, described to us a situation in which these three types of interdependence influenced their crew's performance during a rescue operation. They received a call one evening around 9:30 p.m. when an unmanned Jet Ski was discovered floating in Lake Erie. Once alerted, the crew of the *Thunder Cape* began a difficult nighttime search for the missing rider. As it turned out, two men had set off on the Jet Ski earlier that afternoon and, when they lost control, ended up in the lake. Only one man was wearing a life jacket. The other clung to his friend in the cold water while the two of them hoped someone would find them. No one was waiting for the men on shore, and so their absence went unnoticed for hours.

Working with the Joint Rescue Coordination Center in Trenton, Michigan, crews of a Coast Guard Auxiliary vessel, the *Colchester Guardian*, and a United States Coast Guard helicopter joined the search. The helicopter crew played a critical role in finding the abandoned Jet Ski in the dark, and from there, the crews of the two vessels mapped out a search pattern and began to scour the lake's surface. Within about fifty minutes, a rescue worker from the *Colchester Guardian* saw a heat image on a thermal camera and notified the crew of the *Thunder Cape* who were in closer proximity. Lorbetski said that as they got closer, they could hear cries for help. Ryersee described having to carefully navigate the boat in a way that would enable her crew to pull the men from the water without jeopardizing the rescue or the crew members' safety. After eight hours in the water, the two survivors showed signs of hypothermia and were quickly taken to the hospital once they reached the shore (S. Ryersee & J. Lorbetski, personal communication, November 2017).

This example shows a high degree of task, goal, and outcome interdependence. The difficult task of locating and pulling two men out of a vast lake in the dark depended heavily on the coordination and communication of the helicopter crew and the crew of both boats. The interdependent goal was a successful rescue, which members of the coordinating teams all shared, and the outcome reward was highly dependent on collective and coordinated efforts among all team members.

> Little (1990) noted that joint work is about the acceptance of joint responsibility. "Professional autonomy and discretion reside collectively with the faculty; put more forcefully, each one's teaching is everyone's business, and each one's success is everyone's responsibility" (p. 523).

Progress Is Monitored Based on Success Criteria

A final key feature of a mastery environment relates to the way progress is monitored. Mastery cannot be realized in the absence of identifying progress. Therefore, monitoring and evaluating school improvement plans and the status of the implementation of the plan prove just as important as identifying goals. After all, monitoring allows teams to revise plans based on new information. If it becomes evident that a particular strategy is not working, it is important for teams to determine why and adjust their approaches accordingly. If evidence shows that particular strategies are working, this information strengthens collective efficacy.

We can once again compare and contrast the differences between mastery and performance environments to gain a better understanding of this key feature of a mastery environment. In performance environments, progress is often monitored in relation to how other people are doing. Bandura (1993) pointed out that social comparative standards "carry strong efficacy implications" (p. 123) and noted that if teams see themselves surpassed by others, it undermines efficacy, increases erratic analytic thinking, and progressively impairs performance attainments. In mastery environments, performance is monitored in relation to an objective standard (success criteria) as opposed to normative comparisons. The intention here is to determine whether or not teams demonstrated mastery of a certain skill or set of skills. It establishes an important foundation for engaging school teams with the improvement process.

Using an objective standard to monitor progress benefits the team. When done well, success criteria

- provide a shared language between educators, school, and system leaders;

- identify what is valued in school improvement;

- make explicit to the team what evidence of achievement is expected;

- constitute a source of relevant feedback to team members about what is required for improvement;

- support teams in developing a strong self-evaluation capacity, providing them with tools needed to review, refine, and improve their work.

One of us worked extensively with a teacher team recently that was supporting students' improvement in writing. More specifically, the team aimed to help students develop main ideas with sufficient supporting details. For all of the teachers on this team, this was an identified area of student learning need.

There were a number of evidence-based strategies implemented by the team, including using student samples of work (e.g., exemplars, "bump it up" walls) as a resource for learning; using feedback strategically (e.g., task-, process-, and self-regulation-level feedback depending on where the student is in their learning); and working with marker students to provide targeted support and to monitor impact.

The teacher team developed the following success criteria for use in monitoring their progress:

We'll know we are successful when these conditions exist:

- *Exemplars are used (a) to distinguish effective supporting ideas from those that are less effective by both teachers and students and (b) with and by students in order to track and discuss their progress in developing main ideas with sufficient supporting ideas.*

- *Feedback is acted upon by students and teachers. Students received, understood, and used the feedback provided to improve their ability to develop main ideas with sufficient supporting details. Teachers used feedback from students to adjust their instruction.*

- *Student progress can be tracked in relation to teacher practice(s) in order to determine our impact on student outcomes.*

> Martin (2007) noted that "mastery is required to distinguish between salient and unrelated features, to understand what causal relationships are in play, and . . . to analyze a complex problem" (p. 186).

Mastery experiences provide teams with meaningful information about what they are capable of achieving together and become defining moments as collective efficacy-shaping sources for school improvement teams.

In the previous section, we described significant differences between mastery environments and performance environments. The key features of mastery environments included an openness to learning, a mastery orientation toward goal setting, joint work characterized by positive interdependence, and progress monitoring based on success criteria. Mastery experiences provide teams with meaningful information about what they are capable of achieving together and become defining moments as collective efficacy-shaping sources for school improvement teams. As teams recognize that their efforts are paying off, they begin to increase their confidence in their combined capability. The experience of quality implementation, realized through cycles of progressive inquiry, results in a firmly established sense of collective efficacy.

Implications for Practice

As noted previously, the school environment can have a significant effect on the perceptions of teachers, making it pivotal to quality implementation. In the section that follows, we continue to consider the context of the school and turn our attention to creating the conditions for mastery. We outline four key process foci and explain how these elements are reinforced through cycles of progressive inquiry. Teams can create the conditions for mastery by focusing on the four processes outlined below.

Four Key Foci of Mastery Team Experiences

Mastery team experiences are characterized by the following four key foci:

1. A focus on learning together

2. A focus on cause-and-effect relationships

3. A focus on goal-directed behavior

4. A focus on purposeful practice

A Focus on Learning Together

Learning in organizations does not happen in isolation; it is constructed socially and contextually. However, just providing a time and a location for teams to come together does not guarantee that learning will happen. Professional learning—the kind with the goal of achieving quality implementation—requires more than just time and space for teachers to meet. As noted earlier, quality implementation involves a critical mass of people learning how to apply strategies, assessing impact relative to predetermined success criteria, understanding what worked and what didn't and why within respective contexts, and then making the necessary adjustments. This is the type of collaboration that is characteristic of joint work. In collaborative settings, teams are more likely to engage in joint work when structures (such as the spiral of inquiry, lesson study, and/or microteaching) and protocols are in place.

Progressive inquiry is the methodology that supports collaboration characteristic of joint work. It involves collaboration (learning together) and inquiry (examining teacher and student learning in search of deep understanding of evidence of impact). Readers will recall that *inquiry* is characteristic of an open-to-learning stance, while *advocacy* is characteristic of a knowing stance. Throughout progressive inquiry cycles, as teams assess impact in relation to strategies used and resulting outcomes, it becomes difficult to continue to advocate for approaches that did not produce the expected outcomes. In this sense, progressive inquiry can have profound effects.

Readers will also recall that the relationship between collective efficacy and performance is maximized when there is positive interdependence among team members (Gully et al., 2002). Progressive inquiry methodology promotes positive interdependence. The efforts of each teacher benefit not only the individual but also everyone on the team. The key to positive interdependence is committing to personal success as well as the success of every other teacher on the team. When teams learn together about what worked and what did not in relation to improving outcomes for students, it results in innovative and lasting change.

> *Lindsley et al. (1995) noted that increasing "collective efficacy in the absence of learning can lead to overconfidence" (p. 651).*

A Focus on Cause-and-Effect Relationships

In *The Power of Moments*, Heath and Heath (2017) explore why certain experiences have extraordinary impact. In trying to figure out what makes experiences memorable and meaningful, the Heath brothers noted that "moments of insight deliver realizations and transformation" (p. 132). In schools, these moments of insight occur when cause-and-effect relationships are made explicit. The relationship seems obvious and simplistic—that teaching causes learning—however, Reeves (2010) argued that causes become irrelevant in environments where only effects matter. In many school improvement initiatives, educators are more interested in results (effects) than what caused those results (deep implementation of evidence-based strategies). The methodology of progressive inquiry shines a light on the cause-and-effect relationship between teaching and learning, and these moments of insight become memorable mastery experiences for school improvement teams.

Teacher learning influences student learning and achievement. Put simply, students get better when teachers get better—and teachers get better when they come to think, know, and understand practice differently in a demonstrable area of student learning need (Katz, Dack, & Malloy, 2018). Progressive inquiry methodologies create the conditions for teachers to make the link between their collective actions and student outcomes. The structures involve teachers coming together to tackle challenges of professional practice by questioning what they already know and do in an area of demonstrated student learning need. Most importantly, structures require that teams consider whether or not the evidence shows that their actions have had an effect on student learning.

The link between collective efficacy and increased student achievement is not automatic as teams seek to understand why a particular outcome occurred. Causal attributions play a key role (Bandura, 1998). The impact of mastery experiences on collective efficacy will vary depending on whether accomplishments are ascribed to the team's effort or to other causes. Faulty appraisals sometimes occur in schools. During cycles of progressive inquiry, however, educators' attributions often shift from external causes toward more specific, teacher-implemented instructional actions as explanations for achievement gains. Gallimore, Ermeling, Saunders, and Goldenberg's (2009) research confirmed that teachers moved from assumptions such as "I planned and taught the lesson, but they didn't get it" to beliefs such as "You haven't taught it until they have learned it" (p. 8). Our many experiences in leading progressive inquiry confirm this finding.

> When teams regard themselves as highly efficacious, they "ascribe their failures to insufficient effort; those who regard themselves as inefficacious attribute their failures to low ability" (Bandura, 1993, p. 128).

A Focus on Goal-Directed Behavior

Goal-directed behavior is another key focus for teams in creating the conditions for mastery in schools. Team-level goals encourage performance strategies that foster collaboration, while individual goals encourage strategies that maximize individual performance (Gully et al., 2002). Therefore, it is important for goals to be set and shared by teams rather than at the individual level. Goals, once adopted as part of a particular improvement strategy, guide a team's approach to their work as well as to their thoughts, efforts, and performance. Earlier in this chapter, we described mastery goal orientations as a key feature of mastery environments and contrasted mastery goals and performance goals. Here we revisit these two goal orientations and further consider the relationship between the two.

> *Bruce and Flynn (2013) found that teachers engaging in a collaborative inquiry over a three-year period felt empowered to make instructional decisions together and that the learning design had a "positive impact on teacher beliefs about their abilities to help students learn" (p. 704).*

In an era of performance-driven demands, school improvement goals are largely performance oriented. For example, it is typical for schools to have goals similar to the performance goal stated below:

> Eighty-nine percent (89%) of our junior students will achieve benchmark on the Student Assessment of Growth and Excellence (SAGE) Test by the end of this academic year.

As noted earlier, however, research in classrooms has demonstrated many negative effects of performance goals on learning, including the withdrawal of effort when encountering difficult tasks and lack of intrinsic interest. In contrast, the classroom research on mastery goals demonstrates that they orient students toward acquiring new skills and tackling difficult challenges.

The same holds true regarding goal-directed behavior in businesses as well. Upon examining the outcomes of performance goals versus mastery goals, Seijts and Latham (2005) argued that performance goals can have adverse effects on results in business organizations. The researchers studied the effects of performance goals and mastery goals in a complex business simulation where people were randomly assigned to one of the two conditions. There were four key findings:

1. Performance was highest when a specific mastery goal was stipulated.

2. Those assigned to the mastery goal orientation group took the time necessary to acquire the knowledge and perform tasks effectively (taking the time to analyze the task-relevant information that was available to them).

3. Those assigned to the mastery goal orientation group were convinced that they were capable of mastering the task (an increase in efficacy

occurred as a result of discovering effective strategies, whereas a performance goal led to a "mad scramble" for solutions).

4. Those in the mastery goal group had a higher commitment to their goal than did those in the performance goal orientation group (in addition, the correlation between goal commitment and performance was significant).

We are not suggesting that performance goals go by the wayside. In fact, research has demonstrated that *performance goals depend on the level of attainment of mastery goals* (Hidi & Harackiewicz, 2000). Note that in situations that primarily require the acquisition of knowledge and skills, a specific, challenging mastery goal rather than a performance goal should be set (Seijts & Latham, 2005).

For example, a novice rowing crew should consider setting mastery goals rather than a performance goal in terms of learning how to read and respond to wind conditions, judge boat speed, execute sharp turns, make course corrections, handle emergency stops, and so on. The novice rowing crew must learn basic rowing techniques and boat-handling skills before becoming concerned with attaining a challenging performance outcome (e.g., coming in first place in a racing regatta). Otherwise, the team will not be able to understand the *why* behind the performance outcomes, and when they fall short, they will not know how to adjust accordingly.

Mastery goals result in superior performance because when teams assume a mastery orientation, they are open to learning. The desire to get better and better at something intrinsically motivates teams to figure out why certain things (such as evidence-based strategies) did not work as intended in their context and to pay careful attention to corrective feedback about how to adjust their strategies accordingly. In other words, when school improvement teams assume a mastery orientation, they engage in the progressive inquiry cycles that are required to achieve quality implementation.

> Teachers' sense of efficacy for instructional strategies is positively related to mastery goal orientations (Ciani, Summers, & Easter, 2008).

Research shows that in highly performance-oriented schools, teachers report "significantly less adaptive motivational beliefs, lower community, and more performance-oriented instruction than teachers in a low performance-oriented school" (Ciani et al., 2008, p. 533). These researchers also found that in high schools where performance goals predominated, collective teacher efficacy was low.

A Focus on Purposeful Practice

Purposeful practice is also important for teams wishing to create the conditions for mastery in schools. Only practice builds proficiency in new skills. What is important to consider is the type of practice in which teams engage. Katz, Dack, and Malloy (2018) draw on the expertise research to underscore the relationship between a special kind of practice—purposeful practice and improvement. The four key elements of purposeful practice are narrow goals, a specific area of focus, a clear plan about how to reach the goals, and how to monitor progress (Ericson & Pool, 2016). Katz, Dack, and Malloy (2018) noted that there is no reason to expect significant improvement to occur "without specific, deliberate efforts to improve using purposeful practice" (p. 65).

As noted above, narrow goals are an important aspect of purposeful practice. Revisiting the example of the rowing crew shared above, narrow goals might sound like these:

- Land ten emergency stops in a row without making any mistakes.

- Achieve twenty error-free accelerations to race pace by improving start sequence.

- Increase in-time strokes from twenty-five to thirty strokes per minute to thirty to thirty-five strokes per minute.

When teams are engaged in purposeful practice, they cannot be easily distracted, hence, it is focused. Feedback is integral to monitoring. In regard to teacher teams, feedback can come from a variety of sources including the team itself and/or a trusted, credible other—perhaps a coach or an administrator. However, the most important source of feedback for teacher teams comes from the students they are serving. After completing his first synthesis of research, John Hattie (personal communication, July 2017) realized that feedback was not only something that teachers provided to students but also that it was actually *more powerful* when teachers *received* feedback from their students. Feedback from students to school improvement teams includes information about what students know, understand, and don't understand. It includes information about students' misconceptions, what errors they make, and when they're not engaged. When school improvement teams receive feedback from students and use it to make purposeful adjustments in their practice, learning is enhanced.

Finally, purposeful practice requires that teams step out of their comfort zones and push themselves beyond what they are already capable of doing. This requires the type of creative problem solving that results from engagement in progressive inquiry. Progressive inquiry helps teams remain focused and goal driven based on the desire to improve an identified student learning need. With this comes discomfort. However, with conceptual change, discomfort is necessary. Conceptual change requires that our beliefs or practices are "called into question and challenged in ways that require a revision to what we think, believe, know, and do" (Katz, Dack, & Malloy, 2018, p. 20). Katz and his colleagues pointed out that the "experience of cognitive discomfort is not an unfortunate consequence of new learning; it is an essential prerequisite of new learning" (2018, p. 20).

In Conclusion

When teams form judgments about their future capabilities, they draw on previous experiences. Past experiences provide teams with authentic evidence of whether or not they have what it takes to succeed. When teams meet with success, they come to expect that they can repeat successful performances. This is defined as a mastery experience. Mastery environments, which are favorable to fostering efficacy and achieving quality implementation, show stark contrast to performance environments. Unfortunately, many elements of performance environments exist in schools today (e.g., a heavy reliance on performance-oriented goals).

Improvement teams focus on learning together, cause-and-effect relationships, goal-directed behavior, and purposeful practice in order to create the conditions for mastery in schools. Progressive inquiry provides the methodology for teams to engage in joint work while examining the cause (deep implementation of evidence-based strategies) for improvement (increase in student achievement). These moments of insight become memorable mastery experiences for school improvement teams and strengthen collective efficacy as a result. For complex tasks such as teaching and learning, mastery goals orient teams toward acquiring new skills, trying to understand their work, and improving their collective capacity. Mastery goals are instrumental to quality implementation, which requires learning about what worked and what didn't work and why within respective contexts, and then making the necessary modifications. Mastery goals help focus teams' attention on the learning needed in order to master tasks and are far more effective for supporting quality implementation of new strategies than performance goals. Finally, mastery is built through purposeful practice that is designed to improve a particular area of need. When teams focus their efforts in these four areas, they help to create the conditions for mastery as a source for strengthening collective teacher efficacy.

In the next chapter, we will take a closer look at vicarious experiences as a source of collective efficacy and discuss how to improve the quality of observational learning in ways that enhance observations as an efficacy-shaping source.

TIME FOR REFLECTION

1. To what degree are the key features of mastery environments present in your classroom, school, and/or district?

2. Who is accountable for the quality of professional learning in your school and/or district?

3. Which of the four focus areas is a strength for your team? Which is an area for improvement? How might your team go about improving this area?

CHAPTER 5

LEARNING VICARIOUSLY

People often say that seeing is believing, and it turns out that they are right! In the previous chapter, we examined mastery experiences, which are the most significant source of collective efficacy because they are based on first-hand experiences. Here, we turn our attention to the second most significant source of collective efficacy: vicarious experiences. In psychology, vicarious experiences are defined as the process of learning behavior through observation rather than through direct experience. Vicarious experiences happen when teams (or individual teachers) gain knowledge or information about a strategy, skill, or approach to improving student learning by seeing it performed by others. Vicarious experiences, as a source of efficacy, are important not only at an individual level but for teams as well, as evidenced by the experiences of a team of primary teachers recounted in the example below.

Learning by Observing

Recently, we witnessed firsthand how collective efficacy strengthens through vicarious experiences. A team of primary teachers engaged in progressive inquiry with the goal of strengthening teaching and learning in mathematics. During one cycle in particular, the team engaged in a form of lesson study. They aimed to develop students' early number sense by helping their students recognize patterns in numbers. Many students in each of their classes struggled to master this skill. The teachers learned about and implemented evidence-based instructional strategies including number talks and a three-part lesson plan. The teachers cocreated lessons that focused on pattern recognition, and one teacher volunteered to teach the lesson while the others observed. The following conversation took place when teachers were asked about how their students benefited from their joint work:

Teacher A: "Our common planning and then observations have made me feel more confident in challenging my students. At the beginning of the year, when you all shared what you had your students doing—in

(Continued)

	my head I thought, 'my kids can't do that,' but through our work together, I have seen otherwise."
Teacher B:	"Yeah, there were times when I felt the lessons might be over my students' heads, but when I saw that *Teacher C's* students could do it, I knew I had to give it a try."
Teacher C:	"It was great to see the lightbulbs go off in the students' heads during the number talks and then see how that paid off in their independent work. It was a great combined effort!"
Teacher A:	"I am confident now that I have a role and that I can come in and contribute to the 'build and explore' (an aspect of the three-part lesson plan) rather than just listen to you guys do it" (Teachers, personal interviews, January 24, 2018).

These teachers re-informed and adjusted their mathematics instruction based on their collaborative planning and classroom observations. Their joint work accounted for positive consequences in their classrooms and for their students' learning. Their collective efficacy also strengthened, based on observing increases in students' understanding that resulted from the quality implementation of their collaboratively planned three-part lessons. In addition, Teacher A's increased knowledge about her colleague's practices helped to create a shift in her expectations for her own students. She attributed successes (measured by increases in students' understanding) to the fact that "we had the opportunity to talk and see each other teach" and that their collaboration and classroom observations "made us question and explain what we do" (Teacher A, personal interview, January 24, 2018).

In this chapter, we provide additional examples of vicarious experiences and describe their key features. We also discuss implications for practice and share considerations for tapping into vicarious experiences as a source of collective efficacy.

Key Features of Vicarious Experiences

Vicarious experiences, the second most potent source of collective efficacy, occur through observation. When desire is created in individuals and/or teams to replicate the behavior they have seen modeled by others, this desire generates the vicarious experiences. The vicarious influence of observational experiences, however, is determined by factors including similarity (individuals and teams view a model as alike to themselves and/or their own experiences in key ways) and reinforcement (the observation of positive outcomes of the modeled behavior). Furthermore, additional factors including attention, retention, reproduction, and motivation contribute to the degree to which the observed behavior gets translated into practice. To foster vicarious experiences that deliver on their potential as an efficacy-shaping source, it is important to understand how each of these factors comes into play.

Similarity

The more similar the context, challenge, or task at hand to the observation team's lived experiences, the more influential the vicarious experience will be in fostering a sense of efficacy in observers. In the example of the primary mathematics teachers recounted at the beginning of this chapter, this condition was present. The students in the classroom where the three-part math lesson was modeled came from the same community as the students in the observer's classrooms. Some students in all of the classrooms struggled with the skill of recognizing patterns in math. In addition, the experience was alike in the fact that the teachers were required to teach the same mathematics curriculum, had access to the same resources, and were preparing to teach the same co-planned lesson.

> "Seeing people similar to oneself succeed by perseverant effort raises observers' beliefs in their own abilities" (Bandura, 1998, p. 54).

Reinforcement

Reinforcement influences collective efficacy through peer observations. Behaviors are reinforced when accompanied by positive consequences. Positive reinforcement increases the chances that the observed teacher's actions will be replicated by the observers. In the example of the primary mathematics teachers, reinforcement was strengthened when the observing teachers witnessed the positive consequences ("lightbulbs go off in students' heads") in student learning. Positive consequences can be externally reinforced (e.g., when teachers receive approval from peers and/or administrators) or internally reinforced (e.g., teachers' feelings of accomplishment and satisfaction). In this respect,

> "Observing one perform activities that meet with success does, indeed, produce greater behavioral improvements than witnessing the same performances modeled without any evident consequences" (Bandura, 1977, p. 197).

both clear outcomes and the successful execution of teaching strategies make up important aspects of the observation. The consequences must be evident. We will discuss the role of success criteria as it relates to clear outcomes later in this chapter.

Attention, Retention, Reproduction, and Motivation

Besides similarity and reinforcement, other factors influence vicarious experiences. Bandura (1977) identified four additional processes that intervene during observations to determine whether or not the modeled behavior will be learned by the observers. These are attention, retention, reproduction, and motivation.

- **Attention** refers to the extent to which salient features of the teaching and learning experience are noticed.

- **Retention** refers to how well the steps in the execution of the strategies or teaching approaches are remembered.

- **Reproduction** refers to the extent to which the strategies or teaching approaches are delivered as intended.

- **Motivation** refers to the *will or desire* of observers to perform the behavior.

Examples of how a professional learning facilitator worked to strengthen these processes are included in the example that follows.

Strengthening Observations

A redesigned science curriculum was introduced in a school district in one of the western provinces in Canada over one year ago with the expectation that a full transition from the previous curriculum would take place over the course of two years. The redesigned curriculum incorporated inquiry-based approaches to teaching science as a new key feature. Those responsible for the rollout in the schools and in the district office met with a lot of resistance. Some teachers believed that inquiry-based learning was an "add-on" while others felt that they did not have the content knowledge or conceptual understanding necessary to effectively integrate inquiry-based activities into their science classes. Teachers' questions included, How do we make time for inquiry-based learning? If we provide time for students to spend on inquiry, what do we remove from our day?

As part of the professional development designed to support inquiry-based learning, science teachers from all of the elementary schools in the district were brought together throughout the course of the first year. During the face-to-face sessions, the school district's science coordinator modeled ways to incorporate inquiry into science teaching. She posed questions and conducted experiments using materials that could be easily acquired. She drew on what intrigued the participating teachers and also on the things that did not make sense in relation to their current understanding.

The coordinator reproduced charts for teachers that depicted essential elements of inquiry-based learning in order to draw *attention* to the salient features of each stage in the process. Each time the group embarked on an inquiry, the coordinator made sure to draw explicit attention to the fact that the process began with the interests and wonderings of the audience. In fact, she drew explicit attention to each stage using the chart as a visual reference. For example, when she asked the teachers to make predictions, test hypotheses, and/or create conceptual models, she referred to where they were in the inquiry cycle as it was represented on the chart. Her aim was to direct *attention* to the critical aspects of her instruction and not let what she did with intent and purpose go unnoticed by the teachers in the audience.

In addition to teachers directly observing the coordinator perform inquiry-based teaching, participating teams of teachers watched videos of other teachers successfully utilizing inquiry in their classrooms. At opportune moments, the science coordinator would pause the video and point out and/or ask questions regarding critical elements deemed important to inquiry-based teaching and learning. For example, when observing students in the video collecting and recording data, the coordinator paused the video and referred to the section on the inquiry cycle chart that highlighted data collection and recording as a salient feature in the process. This was in an effort to focus *attention* and increase the extent to which the teachers took note of key aspects of teaching and learning as they related to inquiry.

The coordinator also used a mnemonic device, found online, to support teachers' *retention* of the stages in the inquiry cycle. Although it seemed a bit kitschy, teachers found it a helpful strategy when asked to recall the stages in inquiry learning, and as a result, some used it in their own classrooms to support students' retention. In an effort to strengthen *reproduction*, teachers were provided time to co-plan lessons back at their schools. They were also asked to record the alignment between the phases of the inquiry cycle (based on the chart) and various aspects or activities contained in their lesson plans. This requirement was put in place in an effort to help teachers reproduce activities as they had been demonstrated by the coordinator.

At the start of the second year, teachers continued to voice their questions and concerns about the change in practice they were being asked to make. Questions, however, in the second year were less of a personal nature and more about impact, including,

(Continued)

(Continued)

What strategies are the most effective in using an inquiry-based approach in our school? Will inquiry improve our students' ability to draw scientific conclusions? How will inquiry improve students' ability to understand the expectations outlined in the new science curriculum?

During the second year of the rollout, teachers were encouraged not only to co-plan but also to observe their peers using inquiry techniques in their classrooms. Modeling continued during the face-to-face sessions, but rather than the science coordinator leading the demonstrations, teachers volunteered and were asked to pause and draw *attention* to essential elements of inquiry-based teaching when they deemed it appropriate. Models shared through the videos in year two highlighted classroom successes from participating teachers rather than from teachers the audience members did not know. The coordinator had ensured opportunities for teachers to share success stories in an effort to support *reinforcement* and increase *motivation*.

Observing models of success carried out in environments *similar* to their own helped to strengthen the collective efficacy of the elementary science teachers in this school district. As a result, they were willing to experiment with inquiry-based teaching, assess its impact relative to the intended outcomes, learn about what worked and what didn't work and why within their schools and classrooms, and then make the necessary modifications. Drawing *attention* to the salient features, using strategies to increase *retention*, and ensuring close *reproduction* helped teachers in transferring what they had observed into their actual practice. This example shows how the oscillating relationship between collective efficacy and quality implementation contributed to an impactful outcome.

Modeling can take on various forms. Two of the forms in the example of the redesigned science curriculum were (a) effective actual modeling (e.g., the district's science coordinator and later the science teachers themselves demonstrating inquiry-based approaches during the face-to-face sessions) and (b) symbolic modeling (e.g., videotaped examples of teachers utilizing inquiry in their classrooms). Two additional forms of modeling are (c) self-modeling (e.g., teachers videotape their classroom practices and reflect on their performances) and (d) cognitive self-modeling (e.g., teachers imagine themselves performing a classroom practice successfully; Bautista, 2011).

Psychological Safety

In addition to the above factors that influence whether or not observations will result in learned behavior, it is important that teachers feel a sense of psychological safety when engaging in observational learning. When there is a sense of psychological safety, educators feel like valued team members with important contributions to make to team efforts (as Teacher A felt in the anecdote shared at the beginning of this chapter). When team members have psychological safety, teachers feel safe to take risks. They are confident that no one will embarrass or punish them or anyone else for admitting mistakes, posing questions, or offering new ideas. In other words, effective vicarious experiences thrive on trust.

In environments where mistakes carry evaluative threats (such as in performance environments examined in the previous chapter), teams will select tasks that minimize chances of error in order to demonstrate competency at the expense of expanding their knowledge and skills (Bandura, 1993). What we sometimes encounter, in our work in school improvement, are teams (and leaders) hesitant to engage in the adaptive work of quality implementation too early in a relationship because they want to establish trust first. Clearly, trust matters, and attention to building trusting relationships is a necessary and important function of successful teams.

However, one of the big surprises in the literature on trust indicates that you do not actually have to work hard to achieve it early in a relationship. Tschannen-Moran (2013) noted that "in the absence of any warning signs, people pretty readily extend provisional trust because trust is the easier option" (p. 4). Furthermore, Steven Katz and his colleagues (Katz et al., 2009) have shown that enhanced relational trust represents more an outcome of an effective collaboration than an antecedent. Only a minimal amount of relational trust is necessary to encourage teachers to take a chance together if in a supportive environment. Trust builds *while* engaging in the adaptive work necessary for achieving quality implementation.

Later in this chapter, we will consider how protocols help to create a sense of psychological safety for teachers as they engage in peer observations and interdependent work. Since effective vicarious experiences thrive on trust, it is important to ensure that there are structures and protocols in place to help further risk taking and the establishment of trust.

Recently, Google released its results from Project Aristotle (named after Aristotle, based on his famous quote "The whole is greater than the sum of its parts"), detailing the results from a two-year study investigating what makes an effective team (see Duhigg, 2016; Google, n.d.; Rozovsky, 2015).

Teams were defined as working groups that were highly interdependent; various aspects including formal evaluation and sales performance were included when differentiating high-performing teams from low-performing teams. Julia Rozovsky, the lead researcher on this project, reported that what really mattered was not so much *who* was on the team; what mattered was how the team worked together. Rozovsky (2015) listed five keys to a successful team:

1. Psychological safety (the most important feature of an effective team)

2. Dependability (they could count on each other to produce high-quality work on time)

3. Clarity (goals, roles, and execution plans were clear)

4. Meaning (the work was personally important to everyone on the team)

5. Collective efficacy (they believed they had an impact)

   See list at https://rework.withgoogle.com/blog/five-keys-to-a-successful-google-team/

In the section above, we shared factors that influence learning through observation and, hence, influence vicarious experiences as an efficacy-shaping source. These were similarity, reinforcement, attention, retention, reproduction, and motivation. In addition, psychological safety was identified as an important element to consider in relation to observational learning. In the section that follows, we discuss implications for practice and share considerations for strengthening the factors that influence the degree to which modeled behaviors come to fruition in the observer's own practice.

Implications for Practice

School environments can be shaped to include opportunities for collective efficacy-enhancing vicarious experiences. In the section that follows, we continue to consider how to create the optimal conditions for vicarious experiences in schools through observational learning. Strategies for establishing a culture that enables observational learning are shared, including structures that incorporate peer observation as part of their process. The role of protocols is considered along with suggestions to guide observational learning in ways that will help to enable the kinds of vicarious team experiences described throughout this chapter.

Establishing a Culture That Enables Observational Learning

One of the major purposes of observing peers is learning and the development of practice. This requires a mutual commitment to delving into what is required in the adaptive work of figuring out how to meet the various needs of the students in our schools. It is probably not uncommon, however, that for many teachers, the last time they engaged in observational learning was during their preservice teacher training program. And then, the purpose and goals of observing their peers may not have been obvious or explicit to them. For this and other reasons, teachers may initially be reluctant to opening up their own classroom and/or going into a colleague's classroom.

By involving everyone on the team in the planning process, perceived threats can be minimized. It is also less threatening if teachers self-select their team during the first round of peer observations. Once a few teachers have successful experiences and, through the process, recognize that peer observation is a powerful design for professional learning, they can help to spread the practice throughout the school.

Ensuring successful first experiences is important, and there are ways in which observational learning can be strengthened. It is through the sources of collective efficacy, such as vicarious experiences, that individuals and teams become willing to go out on a limb to experiment with *what's supposed to work* in their own schools and classrooms. When they see others meet with success, it builds the confidence needed to go outside their comfort zones and use focused, goal-driven progressive inquiry to improve teaching and learning. Structures and protocols can be used to help peer observation become an established norm in schools. In addition, teams can guide observations in ways to ensure that the vicarious nature of observational learning is capitalized upon. Each of these ideas is expanded upon in the section that follows.

Readers might be interested in the teacher-initiated Twitter movement #ObserveMe. It began with a post of a picture of a sign outside a classroom teacher's door encouraging others to observe him and provide critical feedback. Before long, signs were being shared from around the world from teachers inviting others to provide them feedback to help them improve their instruction and share best practices with each other. Readers can find more information about the #ObserveMe movement on Twitter and by searching the hashtag #ObserveMe on Facebook. (See https://twitter.com/teacher2teacher/status/817778341189066752)

Structures and Protocols for Observational Learning

Structures and protocols can help to support and strengthen observational learning as a core part of teachers' professional learning. In Jenni Donohoo's earlier book, *Collective Efficacy: How Educators' Beliefs Impact Student Learning* (2017), she suggested that tapping into the sources of efficacy is an important characteristic of high-quality professional learning. Unfortunately, it is often a missed opportunity in much of the professional learning that teachers currently experience.

Progressive inquiry designs that support observational learning and hence tap into vicarious sources of efficacy include lesson study, instructional rounds, microteaching, collaborative inquiry, and collaborative assessment of student learning, to name a few. The specifics of each of these designs are beyond the scope of this book, and readers can find many books and facilitator guides on these topics. Note that these designs provide a structure for professional learning communities that helps teams move beyond talking about teaching to quality implementation.

For more information about professional learning designs that include observational learning as a key component, readers can access the following resources:

- *Focus on Teaching: Using Video for High-Impact Instruction* by Jim Knight

- *Lab Class: Professional Learning Through Collaborative Inquiry and Student Observation* by Lisa Cranston

- *Instructional Rounds in Education* by Elizabeth City, Richard Elmore, Sarah Fiarman, and Lee Teitel

---

According to Hattie's Visible Learning[plus] research (2017), micro-teaching has an effect size of 0.88. An effect size emphasizes the difference in the magnitude of given approaches for the purpose of comparison. The larger the effect size, the more powerful the influence. With an effect size of 0.88, micro-teaching (teachers reviewing videos of their lessons) has the potential to considerably accelerate student learning.

Many protocols designed to support observational learning exist. Observation protocols are generally designed to help teams learn from school and classroom visits. They often provide provisions for psychological safety by articulating expected behaviors and actions, thus separating person and practice. As noted earlier, in order to capitalize on vicarious experiences, it is important that team members have a sense of psychological safety. Protocols offer guidelines for conversations, based on norms that everyone agrees on in order to make the dialogue safe and effective (Brown Easton, 2009). There are many observational protocols available online, and we encourage readers to review them and determine as a team which one is best suited for your team's purposes.

Guiding Observational Learning

Guiding observational learning can also help increase the impact of vicarious experiences as efficacy-shaping sources for teams. Next, we review the six factors that influence the degree to which teachers will replicate the actions they see modeled by their peers along with considerations for guiding peer observations in ways that strengthen each factor.

1. Similarity

Key Idea: This factor especially or more readily influences the acquisition of the modeled behavior when the model is viewed by teams as alike to themselves and/or their own experiences in key ways.

To draw out similarities,

- ensure the hosting teacher sets the context for the lesson being observed (e.g., the teacher being observed conveys background information about the students' learning strengths and needs and what has been taught prior); and

- provide the opportunity for observers to scan the environment in order to notice and identify similarities to their teaching experience (e.g., room arrangement, class size, access to resources) and nudge attention toward the similarities that do exist.

Other opportunities for focusing teachers' attention on similarities include matching teachers based on shared

- cohort of students;

- identified area of student learning need (e.g., ability to infer, draw conclusions, etc.);

- subject area and/or discipline;

- focus for instructional improvement (e.g., pacing, lesson structure, questioning techniques, etc.); and

- experience levels that are not too far apart.

In Ontario, designates in school districts have access to the Similar Schools Analyzer. Originally launched by the Literacy Numeracy Secretariat (referred to as Ontario Statistical Neighbors), this information system allows educators to search for "schools like me." Key data elements include standardized test results; demographic information (e.g., urban/rural, residence type, socioeconomic status); and select school programs (special education, etc.), along with additional program information. Schools can identify other schools that are close matches based on specific criteria. These tools exist in other jurisdictions as well. Upon finding similar schools, observational learning can center on successes encountered.

2. Reinforcement

Key Idea: This factor more readily influences the acquisition of the modeled behavior when the positive outcomes of the modeled behavior are observed.

Teams more readily exhibit modeled behavior if it results in the desired outcomes. Therefore, it is important to identify the success criteria for each lesson or unit of study and to focus teachers' observations on students' demonstration of the success criteria.

To ensure greater reinforcement,

- make the success criteria known to the observers,

- build awareness about the impact teachers are having on student learning, and

- provide positive reinforcement by acknowledging the successes experienced.

3. Attention

Key Idea: This factor more readily influences the acquisition of the modeled behavior when the salient features (i.e., right things) of the experience are noticed.

According to cognitive psychologists, attention is not a limitless resource. Many stimuli in different environments distract our attentional resources. It can be difficult to center our focus on just one thing, and paying attention involves ignoring competing information. Managing attentional resources is important if we want observers to notice the salient features of modeled behavior. Therefore, it's important to direct an observer's attention to the right things.

To draw attention,

- ensure the team knows in advance what the specific focus of the observation should be (e.g., articulation of learning intentions, cocreation of success criteria, questioning techniques, etc.);

- have observers take notes describing objectively what they saw; and

- direct observers' attention to the salient features of the lesson as it is unfolding (if at all possible without causing distraction) or after the fact (using the notes taken to spark memory).

Attention can be tricky. In some cases, our attention might be so focused on a particular thing that it causes us to ignore, or miss, other things. A classic example of this is Chabris and Simons's (2011) famous invisible gorilla experiment. During this selective attention test, people were asked to watch a short video of young adults in different-colored shirts passing a basketball. While observing, the audience is asked to keep a silent count of the number of passes made by the adolescents in white shirts. Many observers miss the fact that a gorilla strolls into the middle of the action, thumps its chest, and then leaves the scene after spending nine seconds on screen. The psychological experiment, conducted by Chabris and Simons (2011) while at Harvard University, demonstrated two things: (a) that people miss a lot of what goes on around them, and (b) people have no idea that they are missing so much.

A recent study by Bruton, Mellalieu, and Shearer (2014) demonstrated the effectiveness of group-based observation interventions as a means of increasing collective efficacy in sports teams. The researchers compared the effects of positive, neutral, and negative video footage of a team's performance during the completion of an obstacle course. Collective efficacy increased for individuals viewing the positive footage of their team and decreased for those who viewed the negative footage of team performance.

4. Retention

Key Idea: This factor more readily influences the acquisition of the modeled behavior when the experience is remembered well.

Not only is attention tricky, but memory is too. Too much happens to be able to retain everything we experience in our memories. Willingham (2009) explored the questions, "What makes something stick in memory, and what is likely to slip away?" and noted that "memory is a residue of thought" (p. 54). Simply put, what we remember well is the product of the quality of thinking that we do about something. "Memory is not a product of what you want to remember or what you try to remember; it's a product of what you think about" (p. 53). Therefore, the depth of mental processing comes into play when trying to remember something well. Deeper levels of processing enhance memorability.

So how can we use this information to influence the acquisition of modeled behavior? We must ensure that teams engage in a deep level of processing regarding the techniques or approaches being modeled. For example, a team might observe a lesson that involves a jigsaw strategy. At the surface level, teams might notice that the jigsaw involves the division of labor because information or content is divvied up among the students. Teams might recall the sequence of events including the transition from home groups to expert groups and back to home groups. Teams might also identify the length of time students were provided to discuss content.

At a slightly deeper level of processing, teams might discuss their observations of students' interactions and assess the quality of students' discussions. They might also inquire into the factors that helped in determining the specific content that lent itself to a jigsaw strategy and why. At an even deeper level of cognitive processing, observers might analyze the jigsaw strategy, then compare and contrast it in relation to Johnson and Johnson's (1987) five basic elements of cooperative learning. For example, what elements of the jigsaw required individual accountability? What elements required positive interdependence?

Johnson and Johnson (1987) noted five basic elements that distinguished cooperative learning from other forms of group learning. These are

- positive interdependence,

- individual and group accountability,

- interpersonal and small group skills,

- face-to-face interaction, and

- group processing.

To increase retention, encourage deep processing. Research has shown the positive effect of cooperative learning methods, including the jigsaw, on various student outcomes including liking school, self-esteem, reduction of prejudices, and increases in students' self-efficacy (Darnon, Buchs, & Desbar, 2012). According to Hattie's (2017) Visible Learning[plus] research, the jigsaw has an effect size of 1.29. To encourage deep processing, explore some of the findings and suggestions from cognitive science including the following (adapted from Sawyer, 2006):

- Ensure that observers relate new ideas and concepts to their previous knowledge and experiences.

- Ask observers to identify patterns and principles underlying the pedagogy.

- Ask teams to draw conclusions about student learning based on evidence gathered during observations.

- Help teams determine cause-and-effect relationships.

- Ask team members to share reflections about their own understandings and identify common understanding.

- Ask teams to reflect on their shared process of learning.

5. Reproduction

<u>Key Idea:</u> This factor readily influences the acquisition of the modeled behavior when the strategies or approaches are replicated just as they were effectively demonstrated.

Marzano (2012) explained why the reported effect sizes of different instructional strategies varies from year to year and from researcher to researcher. By analyzing video recordings of teachers using strategies, Marzano noticed different levels of implementation ranging from beginning level (in which the teacher had little fluency with the strategy, which therefore had little effect on student learning) to an innovating level (in which the teacher is so familiar with the strategy that he or she is able to adapt it to meet specific student needs). The message here is, do not abandon strategies too soon. Teachers need multiple opportunities to see them and practice them in order to understand how to adapt them to meet the various learning needs of students. Guidance includes helping teachers reproduce strategies using the gradual release sequence described below.

To improve reproduction, provide multiple opportunities for observation and reproduction using a gradual release sequence (Meichenbaum, 1977):

- *Demonstration by model*—showing the behavior

- *Modeling with overt guidance*—the observer performs the same actions while talking aloud and being coached

- *Modeling with overt self-guidance*—the observer performs the actions without the guidance of the coach or teammate

- *Modeling with faded self-guidance*—the observer performs the actions while whispering what is happening

- *Modeling with covert self-guidance*—the observer performs the actions while mentally noting what is happening

6. Motivation

<u>Key Idea:</u> This factor more readily influences the acquisition of the modeled behavior when observers have the *will* and *desire* to replicate the strategies.

Motivation is rooted in people needing and wanting to know and learn. Wang, Ertmer, and Newby (2004) designed a study to explore how vicarious learning experiences and goal setting influenced preservice teachers' self-efficacy for technology integration. They found the most powerful significant effect occurred when both vicarious learning experiences and goal setting were present compared to when only one of the two factors was present. Progressive inquiry, as a professional learning methodology, helps to create the demand that drives teams' motivations.

When professional learning is embedded in daily practice (such as progressive inquiry), it becomes more relevant for teachers because the dilemmas they encounter every day become the impetus for the inquiry. The inquiry helps to instill the will and desire to learn.

Motivation is affected not only by people wanting to know but also by other factors, as noted previously, including goals and efficacy. More, a team's expectation of success and the value it places on the goal also come into play. This view of motivation is referred to as the *expectancy-value* model (Wigfield & Eccles, 2002). Teams need to have some expectation of success and to assign the task at least some positive value; otherwise, they will not be motivated at all.

To foster motivation,

- help teams identify dilemmas (related to student learning needs) and pose questions about the dilemmas,

- help teams set mastery goals (as outlined in the previous chapter),

- note the team's opportunities for success, and

- ensure the team sees the value in the task in relation to accomplishing their goals.

In Conclusion

Vicarious experiences are the second most potent source shaping a team's collective efficacy. When learning how to execute strategies by watching the performance of their colleagues, teachers develop the confidence and the staying power required to realize quality implementation. In this chapter, we examined key features of vicarious experiences and provided examples of how teams could be guided in an effort to strengthen observational learning. Peer observations help to increase teachers' knowledge about each other's work and focus collaboration on instructional improvement.

In the next chapter, we focus on both social persuasion and affective states as efficacy-shaping sources and discuss how teams can use theories of persuasion to increase collective efficacy.

TIME FOR REFLECTION

1. To what degree are the key features of vicarious environments present in your classroom and/or school/district?

2. If you knew that a colleague would come into your school or classroom, whom would you ask in, what would they do while they were there, and what would you want the conversation to sound like afterward?

3. What are some immediate steps your team can take to strengthen observational learning in your school?

CHAPTER 6

CONVINCING TEAMS THAT THEY HAVE WHAT IT TAKES

As noted throughout this book, achieving quality implementation of promising evidence-based practices presents a challenge in many schools and districts, and collective efficacy is a promising driver in creating the right kinds of organizational professional learning conditions (i.e., progressive inquiry) that will help us get there. In the previous two chapters, we introduced mastery experiences and vicarious experiences as sources of collective efficacy. Here, we share two additional interconnected sources, social persuasion and affective states. In the vignette shared below, a team of high school English teachers struggles to help their students act upon the evidence-based practice of feedback.

A Case of Helping Students Receive and Act Upon Feedback

It is the second Professional Learning Community (PLC) meeting for the new school year for a team of English teachers in a large high school. During their first PLC meeting, they identified *structuring an argument* as a common student learning need, and all agreed that it was of high importance to address the difficulties students experienced when writing argumentative essays. The teachers shared and voiced a common frustration: that their students did not pay attention to the written feedback they provided and that students had a hard time deciphering the editing codes they used to indicate needed corrections. The team of teachers shared some of the strategies they were currently using including the use of anchor charts, more written feedback, and one-on-one conferencing. Regardless of these strategies, students continued to pay little attention to the feedback. The team ended the meeting by articulating the following question to

According to Hattie's (2017) Visible Learning^plus research, feedback has an effect size of 0.70.

(Continued)

(Continued)

guide its professional inquiry: How can we help students receive and act upon feedback in order to improve their written arguments?

A marker student is a student who has been identified by the teacher, usually a student of interest who might need some extra support and whose progress will be examined by the members of the PLC over time. They are often used as a proxy for a wider group of students.

At the third meeting, teachers brought students' essays and engaged in moderated marking. They used a rubric to grade selected "marker" students' work. They wrote specific comments in the margins to help students move to the next level of proficiency, marked editing codes matching the ones on the anchor charts that hung in their classrooms, and assigned a final grade at the top of the page.

In an attempt to be very purposeful in providing feedback back in their classrooms, teachers provided time for students to examine the graded rubric and read the comments and encouraged students to use the feedback to improve their writing. They reviewed the editing codes and offered the students in their classes the opportunity to resubmit their essays. A common observation was that most of the students compared grades with their friends, filed the papers away, and moved on to a different assigned task.

When the English teachers met again, they continued to express frustrations that students did not take the time to decipher the editing codes, nor did they use the written feedback to revise or improve their writing. They casually observed that the students' preoccupation with the numerical grade seemed to shut down any real consideration of the feedback in a formative sense. That said, the teachers continued to grade the papers as before, even though they believed that the grade drew students' attention away from the written feedback. They had discussed this in the past and agreed that the most advantageous time to assign a grade happened during summative assessments. They concluded their meeting by producing a common prompt for students and agreeing to reteach the structure of an argument the following week.

The teachers continued to grade the papers as before, even though they believed that the grade drew students' attention away from the written feedback.

A couple of weeks later, teachers brought additional samples of student work from the same marker students to their PLC meeting. While assessing the students' arguments, teachers noted that many students made the same common errors that they had made on their previous assignment. Again, the team agreed upon the appropriate level on the rubric, provided written comments, and marked editing codes where needed, and although the intention was formative assessment, the teachers continued to record a grade on the top of the students' written products. The meeting concluded with teachers sharing the different strategies and resources they used to teach students about the structure of an argument in each grade.

While a lot of sharing and exchanging of ideas occurred among the members of the PLC, the English teachers were not seeing improvements in most students' writing. This PLC, along with many others we have observed in the field, failed to achieve quality implementation of formative feedback practices. Remember, we define quality implementation as a process through which the evidence-based promises of improvement-oriented interventions get realized in practice. The problem occurred with the implementation, not with the promising practices of feedback-driven formative assessment. While the PLC continued to talk about *planning* and *acting*, the members spent little time *assessing* and *reflecting* when it came to their own (not the students') practices. In other words, the L in PLC was missing. And as Katz and Dack (2013) remind us, real professional learning requires a *permanent* change in thinking and behavior for the adults as well!

Social Persuasion and Affective States: Two Additional Sources of Collective Efficacy

Readers will recall that with collective efficacy firmly established, teams befriend the dissonance they feel when trying to enact something they haven't done before because that feeling indicates a real change (Katz & Dack, 2013). Social persuasion and affective states are two additional sources that influence collective efficacy. Affective states refer to the feelings and emotions that surface within individuals and teams when faced with challenging situations, and they can be either positive or negative. Positive affective states include enthusiasm, joy, hope, and contentment. Negative emotions, such as discomfort, apprehension, and frustration, can lead to avoidance when efficacy is lacking. Social persuasion occurs when teams are led, through suggestion, into believing and/or acting differently, and it works by tapping into affective states.

Haidt (2006) suggested an effective metaphor when he compared an individual's affective states to that of an elephant and equated people's rational sides to the rider atop the elephant. Even though the rider holds the reins and seems to be in charge, that control is precarious. Given the fact that the sheer size of the elephant overmatches the rider, any time the elephant wants to go in a direction different from the rider's, the elephant overpowers the rider. Heath and Heath (2010) popularized Haidt's metaphor in their book *Switch: How to Change Things When Change Is Hard* and pointed out that the "weakness of the elephant, our emotional and instinctive side, is clear" (p. 7). There are many instances when the elephant overpowers the rider. "Changes often fail because the rider simply can't keep the elephant on the road long enough to reach the destination" (Heath & Heath, 2010, p. 7). On the other hand, the rider also has flaws in the fact that through our rational side, people and teams can become indecisive and spin their wheels (much like the team of English teachers described earlier who became trapped in a cycle of plan-act, plan-act). Haidt (2006) noted that if you really want to change things, you must appeal to the elephant as well as the rider, and it is our contention that when we engage in the seemingly intellectual work of learning about evidence-based practices, we tend to ignore the elephant. And then as a consequence, good rational intentions hit an implementation road-block when practices meet context. Heath and Heath (2010) pointed out that if you reach the riders on your team but not the elephants, "team members will have understanding without motivation" (p. 8). In other words, if you want to influence beliefs, values, and attitudes in order to engage in authentic progressive inquiry, you must engage the elephant.

The type of persuasion we are referring to with respect to its efficacy-enhancing potential is not accidental or coercive. It does not happen by chance, nor is it forceful or threatening. It is fundamentally intentional and communicative. In order for social persuasion to capitalize on its efficacy-enhancing potential, it must be deliberate, ongoing, and sufficiently focused on the affect (the elephant) to convince teams to take the kinds of responsible risks associated with real improvement.

Using Social Persuasion to Influence Collective Efficacy

The psychologist Kurt Lewin famously asked the question, does it work in theory? Theories are fundamentally practical, and in this chapter, we outline three helpful theories that guide us into understanding how social persuasion works. The first theory capitalizes on the dissonance teams experience when they become aware of the gap between their beliefs and their practices. Once teams become aware that a misfit exists between what they *believe in* and what they *actually do*, it creates discomfort. Human beings are predisposed to not like discomfort, so they work to alleviate it by creating better alignment between their beliefs and practices. The second theory, social judgment theory, takes preexisting attitudes into account and suggests that those trying to persuade must consider the preexisting attitudes the audience holds. The final theory concerns the persuasive power of storytelling. Narratives engage people through the affect (the elephant) and therefore can be used to persuade teams to try something new. Knowing how each works can benefit those wanting to socially persuade teams.

Cognitive Dissonance

When teams recognize that certain gaps exist between their beliefs (what they value) and their actions (what they do), this realization creates an uncomfortable feeling—a dissonance. In reaction to this discomfort, teams will change their behavior to be more in line with their beliefs. Let's return to the team of English teachers and their attempts at helping students act upon feedback (shared in the vignette at the beginning of this chapter) to illustrate this theory further.

A Case of Helping Students Receive and Act Upon Feedback (Continued)

The English teachers met numerous times, moderated student work, retaught content, and provided feedback to students; yet students were not revising their written assignments, and little improvement was noted. Readers will recall the PLC was caught in a cycle of planning and acting but not doing much assessing and reflecting in regard to their own practices. This changed when a well-liked and respected teacher (we refer to her as "Teacher C" below) posed a couple of critical questions that helped to break this cycle. Below is the discussion that ensued:

Teacher A: These students just aren't motivated to revise their writing. No matter how much feedback I give, most of my students are done with the assignment once they get it back.

Teacher B: The same thing is happening with my students, and even if I conference individually with them, when I can find the time to do that, it still doesn't make a difference. They just don't want to go back to their writing, even if I give time during class.

Teacher A: I know we've talked about this a lot, and we all agree that once students see the grade it's "game over."

Teacher C: So why do we continue to put the grade on the students' papers? If we *believe* the grade on the paper prevents students from acting on the feedback, why do we continue to record the grade? Isn't this formative assessment that we're trying to convey anyway?

Studies show that there are often inconsistencies between teachers' beliefs and classroom practices. What teachers *believe* is best practice does not necessarily become manifested in their daily work. Teacher C helped to expose the gap between the team teachers' *beliefs* about effective feedback and their feedback *practices* by posing the critical question, If we *believe* the grade on the paper prevents students from acting on the feedback, why do we continue to record the grade?

The above example illustrates what a number of research studies have demonstrated: frequent inconsistencies between teachers' beliefs and classroom practices. For example, Watkins (n.d.) found that although teachers *believed* that fostering student autonomy was advantageous to improving student outcomes, the structures they set up in their classrooms allowed very few opportunities for students to exercise any individual autonomy. Salteh and Sadeghi (2015) found inconsistencies between what writing teachers said they valued in student writing and the feedback they provided. For example, when suggesting revisions, most of the feedback related to surface revisions including spelling, tense, and punctuation, although teachers placed greater value on things such as organization and ideas.

In another example, Lee's (2008) research revealed inconsistencies between teachers' beliefs about effective feedback and the feedback they provided to their students. Lee (2008) investigated teachers' actual written feedback and compared it against their self-described beliefs and values. The researcher found that teachers tended to correct and locate errors for students even though they *believed* that through feedback, it would be more beneficial for students to learn to correct and locate their own errors. Teachers' feedback also demonstrated that they responded mainly to weaknesses in student writing even though they *believed* that feedback should cover both strengths and areas for improvement. Also, similar to the English teachers' experiences in the vignette above, Lee's (2008) study revealed that teachers frequently used error codes even though they *believed* students had a limited ability to decipher the codes.

A helpful strategy we use to expose the gaps between beliefs and practices, in an effort to create cognitive dissonance, is a dual-scale questionnaire. James and Pedder (2006) designed the dual-scale questionnaire for the purpose of shedding light on differences between the value teachers place on certain practices and the frequency in which valued practices are enacted. In the questionnaire, teachers are asked to make two kinds of responses (see Figure 3). The first references whether particular practices are valued (from *not important* to *crucial*) and the second response uncovers the frequency in which they get implemented in the classroom (from *rarely evident* to *mostly evident*). Although learning goals and success criteria are included as the evidence-based strategies in Figure 3, the questionnaire could easily be redesigned to include statements reflective of other educational practices.

Humans show a remarkable propensity to demonstrate incompatible beliefs and behaviors without being fully conscious of the contradiction. Smokers, for example, will explicitly say that they know smoking is bad for their health, while actually smoking and sharing how much they enjoy it. Once teams become aware of the incongruence between their beliefs and practices, it creates an uncomfortable affect state because of the dissonance. In order to alleviate the discomfort, individuals and teams work to bring their beliefs and practices into alignment.

The extent to which teams and individuals will be susceptible to social persuasion as an efficacy-enhancing source will depend on the issue's importance as well as the degree of discomfort they feel (Dainton & Zelley, 2005). Susceptibility to social persuasion also increases when it comes from a credible and trustworthy other (Bandura, 1998). Creating discomfort through cognitive dissonance is exactly what Teacher C brought about when she helped the team members see the disconnect between what they said they valued and what they did in their practice.

Figure 3 Identifying the Gap: Beliefs and Behavior

How important is this in your current practice?				Description	The school/classroom now		
Not important	Of limited importance	Important	Crucial	Explicitly sharing learning goals and success criteria with students so that they can be used as a point of reference for feedback.	Rarely evident	Sometimes evident	Mostly evident
Not important	Of limited importance	Important	Crucial	Encouraging students to make judgments about the quality of work, based on success criteria during its actual production.	Rarely evident	Sometimes evident	Mostly evident
Not important	Of limited importance	Important	Crucial	Increasing students' ability to self-monitor as an important component of the feedback process.	Rarely evident	Sometimes evident	Mostly evident

Social Judgment Theory

Another useful way to think about how to use social persuasion to influence collective efficacy is social judgment theory. Social judgment theory differs from cognitive dissonance theory in that it focuses on the importance of uncovering preexisting attitudes as a critical starting point for potential persuaders. The theory essentially states that knowing people's attitudes can go a long way in supporting our persuasive efforts. The following vignette provides a practical example that will help us in understanding more about how social judgment theory acts as a source of efficacy-shaping information.

A Case of Note-Taking Versus Note-Making

One of us recently overheard a conversation during a lunch break in a high school. At first, it involved an English teacher and a technology teacher and began with the English teacher asking the technology teacher if he allowed students to take pictures, with their phones, of notes placed on the board. Below is the discussion that followed:

Tech Teacher:	You know I have been thinking about that lately. A student asked me a few weeks ago if he could just take a picture of the whiteboard, and I wouldn't let him. But when I was at home that night, I thought more about it and wondered why not.
English Teacher:	I have thought a lot about it too. The kids ask me all the time, and I won't let them do it.
Tech Teacher:	Well, you know, what I really want is for them to have a record of the note so they have the material to study.
English Teacher:	I know, but they should still be required to write it down themselves.
Tech Teacher:	I was wondering if there is benefit to them transferring from the board to paper or a word processor, and I am not sure. I suppose that by writing it down themselves, they might be more likely to remember it.
English Teacher:	Yes. It is a non-negotiable in my classroom. I project onto a screen, and I require them to record their own notes. It's part of our everyday routine.
Tech Teacher:	I have been letting them take pictures, but then I ask them to do something with it.

English Teacher:	Yeah, I suppose that is okay but, in my class, there are a lot of notes, so having the students write them out is important. Plus, it keeps them quiet for a while.

At this point, the school district's literacy consultant (who was also listening to the teachers' conversation) joined the discussion.

Note-taking is a passive process, while note-making is an active and focused activity in which students review and synthesize ideas for deeper processing. A Cornell Note is an example of a note-making strategy.

Literacy Consultant:	You know, it might not be the best use of students' time to copy notes from a whiteboard in every class. I could share some other strategies with you.
English Teacher:	No. Things are just fine the way they are in my classroom.
Tech Teacher:	I'd be interested in knowing more.

According to Dainton and Zelley (2005), "social judgement theory suggests that knowing a person's attitudes on subjects can provide you with clues about how to approach a persuasive effort" (p. 105). People's attitudes will range from acceptance to rejection. The more the team or individual finds the ideas aligned with their current beliefs, the more likely they are to be persuaded to accept new ideas. The more the team or individual finds the ideas in conflict with their current ideas, the less likely they are to accept them. Finally, there is also a realm of noncommitment. This refers to the times when a team or individual has no real opinion on certain ideas.

The central idea is that people's reaction to the persuasive effort is dependent upon how closely they are positioned along the continuum (Dainton & Zelley, 2005). In other words, acceptance or rejection depends upon how closely the ideas align or conflict with current beliefs. If you feel strongly about something, you are likely to reject anything that does not match your point of view. Ideas will be rejected completely if they fall within the person's latitude of rejection (as evident in the English teacher's position on the topic of note-taking and response to the literacy consultant). Successful persuasion will likely occur only if the message is within an individual's or team's latitude of noncommitment or at the edges of their acceptance (as evident in the tech teacher's willingness to learn more). Had the literacy consultant approached the discussion with an acute awareness of and attention to the English teacher's current attitude about the topic, she may have had more success by building a more "friendly ramp" to the new idea. This might have sounded something like "I agree. Note-taking is very important. I would never suggest that you stop using it in your class. I recently learned about the difference between note-taking and note-making. If you're interested, together we can figure out how to maximize this strategy in your class."

Successful persuasion will likely occur only if the message is within an individual's or team's latitude of noncommitment or at the edges of their acceptance.

Affect is deeply implicated in social judgment theory because of how the ego comes into play (Dainton & Zelley, 2005). If individuals or teams are highly ego involved, they will reject anything that does not match their current point of view. If they are *on the fence* about the topic, they will be more likely to accept new and different ideas (as demonstrated by the tech teacher's willingness to explore alternatives to note-taking in his classroom). In addition, the more teams and individuals believe a topic is important (for example, note-taking was obviously *very important* to the English teacher—probably because she was relying on it as a misguided classroom management strategy), the smaller their latitude of noncommitment. This makes a lot of sense given our example; the English teacher had clearly spent a lot of time thinking about this issue and therefore had a strong opinion about it.

The contrast effect occurs when the differences between points of view are subconsciously exaggerated or minimized.

During these moments of potential persuasion, one of two subconscious effects can occur: an *exaggeration* of differences or a *minimization* of differences. Dainton and Zelley (2005) referred to the exaggeration of differences as the "contrast effect." The English teacher exaggerated the difference between the literacy consultant's ideas and her own. As she walked out of the lunch room, she commented that it would require *a lot* of convincing to get her to change her routine. The opposite, what Dainton and Zelley (2005) referred to as an "assimilation effect," occurs when the receiver minimizes the difference between a messenger's position and his or her own.

Social judgment theory, therefore, states that in order to truly persuade, it is important to know preexisting attitudes and send messages within the team's latitude of noncommitment or at the edges of the team's latitude of acceptance as a way in. If the social persuader sends messages that fall in a receiver's latitude of rejection, he/she will not be successful. However, if the persuader sends messages that are clearly in the team's latitude of acceptance, he/she is only reinforcing what the team already believes.

If the persuader sends messages that are clearly in the team's latitude of acceptance, he/she is only reinforcing what the team already believes.

The Narrative Paradigm

The third theory of how to capitalize on social persuasion to influence collective efficacy involves the use of storytelling. Rutledge (2011) details the psychological power of storytelling and notes that stories engage us through emotion (the elephant), trigger imagination, and connect us and bridge differences. A good narrative can convince school teams of good reasons for engaging in a particular action. In other words, a compelling narrative addresses the elephant.

We aimed to model this throughout this book by creating a narrative that would appeal to the reader's elephant. Stories we shared including "The Bridge Incident" in which Ray Navarro's firefighting team rescued Kelli Groves and her daughters from the car accident (see Preface), Stacy Allison and her team's successful Everest climb (see Chapter 3), and the Thunder Cape crew who rescued the two men who fell off their Jet Ski in Lake Erie (see Chapter 4) all have a very strong emotional appeal. At the same time, they all demonstrate very relevant reasons why team members need to work interdependently in order to succeed. Remember, the relationship between collective efficacy and results is maximized when there is positive interdependence among team members (Gully et al., 2002).

In addition, stories are more likely to be accepted by others when they tap into people's personal narratives and are viewed as having fidelity. The educational stories we shared throughout this book, which included many examples of failed attempts at spreading evidence-based practices by well-intentioned educators, probably resonated with readers because they reflect many educators' lived experiences. Also, because they were described accurately and factually, they are likely to be viewed as having fidelity. Walter Fisher, the American professor who theorized the narrative paradigm, noted that all meaningful communication occurs through storytelling (as cited in Rutledge, 2011). When teams are considering how

Csikszentmihalyi (1990) coined the term "flow" based on studies of happiness and creativity and described flow as individuals being immersed in optimal experience. Flow experiences are characterized by positive affective states such as enjoyment, satisfaction, and contentment. Sandoval et al. (2011) investigated flow experiences at the group level and found that people serve as agents of flow for each other in highly interdependent and interactive situations. Furthermore, the researchers found that collective flow is both a precursor and an outcome of collective efficacy. In other words, when groups experience feelings of enjoyment, satisfaction, and contentment, resulting from their joint work, their sense of collective efficacy increases. With an increase in collective efficacy, groups perceive greater challenges immediately and feel more competent, which impacts their collective flow experience. Therefore, positive affective states that result from collective flow experiences indicate a direct source for building collective efficacy.

to influence collective efficacy, it would be advantageous to integrate stories that are crafted to appeal to people's emotions.

As discussed in this chapter, a team's efficaciousness is influenced through social persuasion and affective states. Knowledge about persuasion can help when needing to move teams to adopt new attitudes or beliefs, or to take action. Persuasion is a tool that works because it is the type of communication that appeals to affect. The three approaches to thinking about persuasion that we've outlined, when taken together, chart a course forward in helping us understand how to intentionally capitalize on social persuasion, in an affectively compelling way, in order to enhance collective efficacy. We encourage teams to consider how they might enact these theories in their efforts to increase collective efficacy among team members.

In Conclusion

This book is about the power of collective efficacy in schools and districts, and we have outlined research that demonstrates that collective efficacy is a significant belief system for improving student outcomes. We have explained that collective efficacy influences student achievement because greater efficacy drives key behaviors that are instrumental to quality implementation. Remember, quality implementation is a process through which evidence-based promises of improvement-oriented interventions get realized in practice. We outlined what teams could do to create mastery environments, strengthen vicarious experiences through observational learning, and use social persuasion that targets affective states as means of fostering collective teacher efficacy. And the key behaviors that prove instrumental to quality implementation are the habits of progressive inquiry—which include evidence-informed, collaborative professional learning processes that follow a disciplined experimentation and hypothesis-testing methodology of plan-act-assess-reflect in context. School improvement depends on the collective belief that the teaching faculty has what it takes to improve student achievement; therefore, teams must be purposeful in their efforts to instill a sense of collective efficacy among all educators in schools and districts.

Cognitive scientists, working on the challenge of knowledge mobilization, have long argued for the value of robust conceptual frameworks. Bransford et al. (2000) have explained that if one aims to be truly competent in an area of inquiry, facts and ideas must be understood within the context of a conceptual framework. Conceptual frameworks organize information. And the more organized the information, the more likely it is to be transferred into applicable situations and used. It is in this spirit, then, that we conclude this book by encouraging readers to revisit the conceptual framework (see Figure 1) that identifies and interrelates the key concepts in this book. It is our hope that in this way we are doing our part to support the quality implementation of the evidence-based practices associated with collective efficacy.

TIME FOR REFLECTION

1. How might your team make use of social persuasion and positive affective states as efficacy-enhancing sources?

2. What might your team do to strengthen professional learning processes in your school?

3. How will your team know when you have reached quality implementation?

REFERENCES

Alvidrez, J., & Weinstein, R. (1999). Early teacher perceptions and later student academic achievement. *Journal of Educational Psychology*, 91(4), 731–746.

Archambault, I., Janosz, M., & Chouinard, R. (2012). Teacher beliefs as predictors of adolescents' cognitive engagement and achievement in mathematics. *The Journal of Educational Research*, 105(5), 319–328.

Balas, E. A., & Boren, S. A. (2000). Managing clinical knowledge for health care improvement. *Yearbook of Medical Informatics*, 9(1), 65–70. doi: 10.1055/s-0038-1637943

Bandura, A. (1977). Self efficacy: Toward a unifying theory of behavioural change. *Psychological Review*, 84(2), 191–215.

Bandura, A. (1993). Perceived self-efficacy in cognitive development and functioning. *Educational Psychologist*, 28(2), 117–148.

Bandura, A. (1997). *Self efficacy: The exercise of control*. New York, NY: W.H. Freeman and Company.

Bandura, A. (1998). Personal and collective efficacy in human adaptation and change. In J. G. Adair, D. Belanger, & K. L. Dion (Eds.), *Advances in psychological science, Vol. 1: Social, personal, and cultural aspects* (pp. 52–71). Hove, UK: Psychology Press.

Bauer, M., Damschroder, L., Hagedorn, H., Smith, J., & Kilbourne, A. (2015). An introduction to implementation science for the non-specialist. *BMC Psychology*, 3(1), 32. Retrieved from https://www.ncbi.nlm.nih.gov/pmc/articles/PMC4573926/

Bautista, N. (2011). Investigating the use of vicarious and mastery experiences in influencing early childhood education majors' self-efficacy beliefs. *Journal for Science Teacher Education*, 22, 333–349.

Boser, U., Wilhelm, M., & Hanna, R. (2014). *The power of the Pygmalion effect: Teachers' expectations strongly predict college completion*. Washington, DC: Center for American Progress.

Bransford, J., Brown, A., & Cocking, R. (Eds.). (2000). *How people learn: Brain, mind, experience, and school*. Washington, DC: National Academy Press.

Brophy, J. (1983). Research on the self-fulfilling prophecy and teacher expectations. *Journal of Educational Psychology*, 76, 236–247.

Brown Easton, L. (2009). *Protocols for professional learning*. Alexandria, VA: Association for Supervision and Curriculum Development.

Bruce, C., & Flynn, T. (2013). Assessing the effects of collaborative professional learning: Efficacy shifts in a three-year mathematics study. *Alberta Journal of Educational Research*, 58(4), 691–709.

Bruton, A., Mellalieu, S., & Shearer, D. (2014). Observation interventions as a means to manipulate collective efficacy in groups. *Journal of Sport and Exercise Psychology*, 36, 27–39.

Cepikkurt, F., & Uluoz, E. (2017). Predictive power of group cohesion and perceived motivational climate for collective efficacy perception in the football teams. *Sport and Society International Journal of Physical Education*, 17(1), 91–97.

Chabris, C. V., & Simons, D. (2011). *The invisible gorilla: How our intuitions deceive us*. New York, NY: Random House.

Ciani, K., Summers, J., & Easter, M. (2008). A top-down analysis of high school teacher motivation. *Contemporary Educational Psychology, 33*, 533–560.

City, E., Elmore, R., Fiarman, S., & Teitel, L. (2009). *Instructional rounds in education: A network approach to improving teaching and learning.* Cambridge, MA Harvard Education Press.

Coburn, C. (2003). Rethinking scale: Moving beyond numbers to deep and lasting change. *Educational Researcher, 32*(6), 3–12.

Cranston, L. (2019). *Lab class: Professional learning through collaborative inquiry and student observation.* Thousand Oaks, CA: Corwin.

Csikszentmihalyi, M. (1990). *Flow: The psychology of optimal experience.* New York, NY: HarperCollins.

Dainton, M., & Zelley, E. (2005). *Applying communication theory for professional life: A practical introduction.* Thousand Oaks, CA: Sage.

Darnon, C., Buchs, C., & Desbar, D. (2012). The jigsaw technique and self-efficacy of vocational training students: A practice report. *Journal of Psychological Education, 27*, 439–449.

Donohoo, J. (2013). *Collaborative inquiry for educators: A facilitator's guide to school improvement.* Thousand Oaks, CA: Corwin.

Donohoo, J. (2017). *Collective efficacy: How educators' beliefs impact student learning.* Thousand Oaks, CA: Corwin.

Donohoo, J. (2018). Collective teacher efficacy research: Productive patterns of behaviour and other positive consequences. *Journal of Educational Change, 19*, 323–345.

Donohoo, J., Hattie, J., & Eells, R. (2018). The power of collective efficacy. *Educational Leadership, 75*(6), 41–44.

Duhigg, C. (2016, February 25). What Google learned from its quest to build the perfect team. *New York Times Magazine.* Retrieved from https://www.nytimes.com/2016/02/28/magazine/what-google-learned-from-its-quest-to-build-the-perfect-team.html

Dweck, C. (2008). *Mindset: The new psychology of success.* New York, NY: Ballantine Books.

Eells, R. (2011). *Meta-analysis of the relationship between collective efficacy and student achievement* (Unpublished doctoral dissertation). Loyola University of Chicago.

Ericson, A., & Pool, R. (2016). *Peak: How to master almost anything.* Toronto, ON: Penguin Canada.

Gallimore, R., Ermeling, B., Saunders, W., & Goldenberg, C. (2009). Moving the learning of teaching closer to practice: Teacher education implications of school-based inquiry teams. *The Elementary School Journal, 109*(5), 1–18.

Goddard, R. (2001). Collective efficacy: A neglected construct in the study of schools and student achievement. *Journal of Educational Psychology, 93*(3), 467–476.

Goddard, R., Goddard, Y., Kim, E., & Miller, R. (2015). A theoretical and empirical analysis of the roles of instructional leadership, teacher collaboration, and collective efficacy beliefs in support of student learning. *American Journal of Education, 121*, 501–530.

Goddard, R., Hoy, W., & Woolfolk Hoy, A. (2004). Collective efficacy beliefs: Theoretical developments, empirical evidence, and future directions. *Educational Researcher, 33*(3), 3–13.

Google. (n.d.). Introduction. *Re:Work.* Retrieved from https://rework.withgoogle.com/print/guides/5721312655835136/

Greenlees, I., Graydon, J., & Maynard, I. (2000). The impact of individual efficacy beliefs on group goal selection and group goal commitment. *Journal of Sports Sciences, 18*, 451–459.

Gully, S., Incalcaterra, K., Joshi, A., & Beaubein, J. M. (2002). A meta-analysis of team-efficacy, potency, and performance: Interdependence and level of analysis as moderators of observed relationships. *Journal of Applied Psychology*, 87(5), 819–832.

Guskey, T. (2000). *Evaluating professional development*. Thousand Oaks, CA: Corwin.

Haidt, J. (2006). *The happiness hypothesis: Finding modern truth in ancient wisdom*. New York, NY: Basic Books.

Hattie, J. (2009). *Visible Learning: A synthesis of over 800 meta-analyses relating to achievement*. New York, NY: Routledge.

Hattie, J. (2017). Visible Learning[plus] [Chart]. Retrieved from https://visible-learning.org/wp-content/uploads/2018/03/VLPLUS-252-Influences-Hattie-ranking-DEC-2017.pdf

Heath, C., & Heath, D. (2010). *Switch: How to change things when change is hard*. Toronto, Ontario: Random House Canada.

Heath, C., & Heath, D. (2017). *The power of moments: Why certain experiences have extraordinary impact*. New York, NY: Simon & Schuster.

Hidi, H., & Harackiewicz, J. (2000). Motivating the academically unmotivated: A critical issue for the 21st century. *Review of Educational Research*, 70(2), 151–179.

James, M., & Pedder, D. (2006). Beyond method: Assessment and learning practices and values. *The Curriculum Journal*, 17(2), 109–138.

Johnson, D., & Johnson, F. (1987). *Joining together: Group therapy and group skills* (3rd ed.). Englewood Cliffs, NJ: Prentice-Hall.

Kao, S., & Watson, J. (2014). The multilevel effects of motivational climate on the collective efficacy in a cheerleading team. *International Journal of Sports Science & Coaching*, 9(4), 593–603.

Katz, S., & Dack, L. (2013). *Intentional interruption: Breaking down learning barriers to transform professional practice*. Thousand Oaks, CA: Corwin.

Katz, S., Dack, L., & Malloy, J. (2018). *The intelligent, responsive leader*. Thousand Oaks, CA: Corwin.

Katz, S., Earl, L., & Ben Jaafar, S. (2009). *Building and connecting learning communities: The power of networks for school improvement*. Thousand Oaks, CA: Corwin.

Knight, J. (2014). *Focus on teaching: Using video for high-impact instruction*. Thousand Oaks, CA: Corwin.

Lee, I. (2008). Ten mismatches between teachers' beliefs and written feedback. *ETE Journal*, 63(1), 13–22.

Lindland, E., Fond, M., Haydon, A., Volmert, A., & Kendall-Taylor, N. (2015). *Just do it: Communicating implementation science and practice*. Frameworks Institute. Retrieved March 3, 2018, from https://www.frameworksinstitute.org/assets/files/evidence_implementation/NIRNreprt_justdoit_2015.pdf

Lindsley, D., Brass, D., & Thomas, J. (1995). Efficacy-performance spirals: A multilevel perspective. *Academy of Management Review*, 20(3), 645–678.

Little, J. W. (1990). The persistence of privacy: Autonomy and initiative in teachers' professional relations. *Teachers College Record*, 91(4), 509–536.

Livingston, S. (2003, January). Pygmalion in management. *Harvard Business Review Classic*, Impact on Productivity section. Retrieved March 11, 2018, from https://hbr.org/2003/01/pygmalion-in-management

Locke, E., & Latham, G. (2002). Building a practically useful theory of goal setting and task motivation: A 35-year odyssey. *American Psychologist*, 57, 705–717.

Locke, E., & Latham, G. (2006). New directions in goal-setting theory. *Current Directions in Psychological Science, 15*(5), 265–268.

Magyar, M., Feltz, D., & Simpson, I. (2004). Individual and crew level determinants of collective efficacy in rowing. *Journal of Sport & Exercise Psychology, 26*, 136–153.

Martin, R. (2007). *The opposable mind: How successful leaders win through integrative thinking.* Boston, MA: Harvard Business School.

Marzano, R. (2003). *What works in schools: Translating research into action.* Alexandria, VA: Association for Supervision and Curriculum Development.

Marzano, R. E. (2012). Art and science of teaching/It's how you use a strategy. *Educational Leadership, 69*(4), 88–89.

Meichenbaum, D. (1977). *Cognitive-behavior modification: An integrative approach.* New York, NY: Plenum.

Moolenaar, A., Sleegers, P., & Daly, A. (2012). Teaming up: Linking collaboration networks, collective efficacy, and student achievement. *Teaching and Teacher Education, 28*, 251–262.

Parks, M., Solmon, M., & Lee, A. (2007). Understanding classroom teachers' perceptions of integrating physical activity: A collective efficacy perspective. *Journal of Research in Childhood Education, 21*(3), 316–328.

Pink, D. (2009). *Drive: The surprising truth about what motivates us.* New York, NY: Penguin.

Reeves, D. (2008). *Reframing teacher leadership to improve your school.* Alexandria, VA: Association for Supervision and Curriculum Development.

Reeves, D. (2010). *Transforming professional development into student results.* Alexandria, VA: Association for Supervision and Curriculum Development.

Robinson, V., Hohepa, M., & Lloyd, C. (2009). *School leadership and student outcomes: Identifying what works and why.* Best evidence synthesis iteration [BES]. Auckland, New Zealand: Ministry of Education.

Rosenthal, R., & Jacobson, L. (1968). *Pygmalion in the classroom: Teacher expectation and pupils' intellectual development.* New York, NY: Holt, Rinehart and Winston.

Rozovsky, J. (2015, November 17). The five keys to a successful Google team. *Re:Work.* Retrieved from https://rework.withgoogle.com/blog/five-keys-to-a-successful-google-team/

Rutledge, P. (2011). The psychological power of storytelling. *Psychology Today.* Retrieved from https://www.psychologytoday.com/us/blog/positively-media/201101/the-psychological-power-storytelling

Salteh, M., & Sadeghi, K. (2015). What writing teachers say and what they actually do: The mismatch between theory and practice. *Journal of Language Teaching and Research, 6*(4), 803–810.

Sandoval, J., Challoo, L., & Kupczynski, L. (2011). The relationship between teachers' collective efficacy and student achievement at economically disadvantaged middle school campuses. *Journal on Educational Psychology, 5*(1), 9–23.

Sawhney, G., Jennings, K., Britt, T., & Sliter, M. (2017, June). Occupational stress and mental health symptoms: Examining the moderating effect of work recovery strategies in firefighters. *Journal of Occupational Health Psychology, 23*(3), 443–456. Advance online publication doi: 10.1037/ocp0000091

Sawyer, K. (2006). The new science of learning. In R. K. Sawyer (Ed.), *The Cambridge handbook of the learning sciences* (p. 4). New York: Cambridge University Press.

Seijts, G., & Latham, G. (2005). Learning versus performance goals: When should each be used? *Academy of Management Executive, 19*(1), 124–131.

Timperley, H., Kaser, L., & Halbert, J. (2014). *Seminar Series 234: A framework for transforming learning in schools: Innovation and the spiral of inquiry*. Melbourne, Australia: Centre for Strategic Education.

Tschannen-Moran, M. (2013). Healthy relationships: The foundation of a positive school climate. *In Conversation, 4*(3), 1–14.

Tschannen-Moran, M., & Barr, M. (2004). Fostering student learning: The relationship of collective teacher efficacy and student achievement. *Leadership and Policy in Schools, 3*(3), 189–209.

Wang, L., Ertmer, P., & Newby, T. (2004). Increasing preservice teachers' self-efficacy beliefs for technology integration. *Journal of Research on Technology in Education, 36*(3), 231–250.

Wang, Y., & Willis, E. (2016). Examining theory-based behavior-change constructs, social interaction, and sociability features of the Weight Watchers' online community. *Health Education and Behavior, 43*(6), 656–664.

Watkins, C. (n.d.). Learners in the driving seat: Leading learning pedagogy. *School Leadership Today, 1*(2), 28–31.

Wigfield, A., & Eccles, J. (2002). *The development of achievement motivation*. San Diego, CA: Academic Press.

Willingham, W. (2009). *Why don't students like school? A cognitive scientist answers questions about how the mind works and what it means for the classroom*. Hoboken, NJ: Jossey-Bass.

INDEX

Equity Beyond Compliance

Resources for Building a Better World

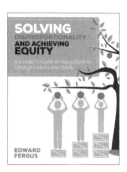

EDWARD FERGUS
Adaptive strategies for systemic change and technical skills for using data to promote equity

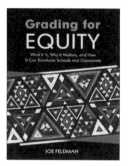

JOE FELDMAN
Richly detailed examples and strategies to make grading more bias-resistant and motivational

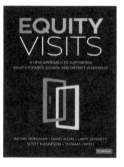

RACHEL ROEGMAN, DAVID ALLEN, LARRY LEVERETT, SCOTT THOMPSON, THOMAS HATCH
An innovative practice to identify and address systemic inequities in instructional practice in classrooms, schools, and districts

H. RICHARD MILNER IV, HEATHER B. CUNNINGHAM, LORI DELALE-O'CONNOR, ERIKA GOLD KESTENBERG
A research-based guide to rethinking classroom management that effectively serves the needs of diverse learners

PAUL EMERICH FRANCE
Practical guidance on enacting humanized personalization to curriculum design, assessment, and instruction

RANDALL B. LINDSEY, KIKANZA NURI-ROBBINS, RAYMOND D. TERRELL, DELORES B. LINDSEY
A resource for creating equitable educational opportunities and more inclusive environments in which differences are embraced

EDDIE MOORE JR., ALI MICHAEL, MARGUERITE W. PENICK-PARKS
Guidance for success in positively shifting outcomes for Black boys and young men by first changing the way school is "done"

ZARETTA HAMMOND
Cutting-edge neuroscience research offering an innovative approach for brain-compatible culturally responsive instruction

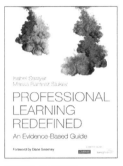

ISABEL SAWYER, MARISA RAMIREZ STUKEY

An elemental analysis of professional learning, providing the tools and framework for systemic shifts in instructional practice

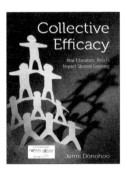

JENNI DONOHOO

Research suggesting that collective efficacy is the number one factor influencing student achievement

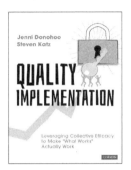

JENNI DONOHOO

Strategies and lessons to help teams achieve quality implementation of evidence-based practices for innovative and lasting change

LAURA BAECHER

A resource explaining how to engage in nonjudgmental, descriptive analysis using video recording to promote reflective practice

JENNIFER ABRAMS

An insightful book offering interactive exercises, sample scripts, and an approach to help realize positive outcomes and confidently lead difficult conversations

DIANE SWEENEY, ANN MAUSBACH

An action-oriented guide providing principals and district leaders with the background, practices, and tools for leading instructional coaching

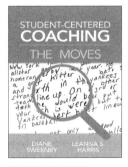

DIANE SWEENEY, LEANNA S. HARRIS

A how-to guide for creating student-centered coaching relationships, addressing the essential coaching moves that every coach needs

JOELLEN KILLION

A guide to help produce an effective, in-depth, results-based evaluation to measure effectiveness and retain stakeholder support

CORWIN
A SAGE Publishing Company

Helping educators make the greatest impact

CORWIN HAS ONE MISSION: to enhance education through intentional professional learning.

We build long-term relationships with our authors, educators, clients, and associations who partner with us to develop and continuously improve the best evidence-based practices that establish and support lifelong learning.